Sex, Ideology and Religion

BY THE SAME AUTHOR:

Education and Knowledge (Routledge and Kegan Paul, 1979)
Teachers and Classes (Routledge and Kegan Paul, 1982)

Sex, Ideology and Religion
The Representation of Women in the Bible

Kevin Harris
Senior Lecturer, School of Education
University of New South Wales

BARNES & NOBLE BOOKS · NEW JERSEY

First published in Great Britain in 1984 by
WHEATSHEAF BOOKS LTD
A MEMBER OF THE HARVESTER PRESS PUBLISHING GROUP
Publisher: John Spiers
Director of Publications: Edward Elgar
16 Ship Street, Brighton, Sussex
and in the USA by
BARNES & NOBLE BOOKS
81 Adams Drive, Totowa, New Jersey 07512

© Kevin Harris, 1984

British Library Cataloguing in Publication Data

Harris, Kevin
   Sex, ideology and religion.
1. Women in the Bible
I. Title
220.8'3054   BS680.W7
ISBN 0-7450-0002-9

Library of Congress Cataloging in Publication Data

Harris, Kevin.
   Sex, ideology, and religion.
   1. Women in the Bible.   2. Sexism in the Bible.
I. Title.
BS680.W7H37   1984   261.8'344   84-12413
ISBN 0-389-20509-5

Typeset in 11 point Bembo by Preface Ltd, Salisbury, Wilts
Printed in Great Britain by Whitstable Litho Ltd, Whitstable, Kent

All rights reserved

To the memory of Mahlah, Noah, Hoglah,
Milcah and Tirzah —

who were instrumental in securing new rights and conditions for women, whose names actually were recorded for posterity, but who seem to have been largely overlooked, forgotten, or remembered only as the daughters of Zelophehad.

Contents

Preface	ix
1 Introduction and explanations	1
The Purpose	1
Why the Bible?	3
(a) The time factor	5
(b) The saturation factor	6
(c) The inspirational factor	8
(d) The susceptibility factor	11
Sources, Translations, Texts and Interpretations	15
On Selection	19
On the Historical Context	24
The Two Testaments	27
Concluding Points	28
2 The Place of Women	30
Introduction	30
The Absence of Women	31
In the Beginning: Woman Was Created Inferior	39
The Paulene Statements: Man to Command and Women to Obey	41
Man to Command and Win Bread: Women to Bear Children	45

Women Are Commodities: to be Given into
   Marriage 53
Violate the Daughter: Then Pay the Father 57
Women Are Commodities: to be Taken, Given
   Away, and Owned Outside of Marriage 58
Women as Sex Objects Offered up to Others 61
Women Are Sub-human 66
Women Need Men for Guidance and Fulfilment 66
Gender Differences under Law and Custom 69
No Greater Shame . . . 75

3 The Characteristics of Women 77
  Introduction 77
  Women Are Silly, Prattlers and Naggers 78
  Women Are Cowardly 81
  Women Are Temptresses and Betrayers 84
  Women Are the Source and Cause of Evil Doings 91
  Women Have Periods 98
  Virgins Are Virtuous; Whores Are Evil 102
  The Good Woman 107
  Women: To Have or Have Not? 109
  Selected Analogies with 'Female Characteristics' 114

4 Conclusion 119

Notes 123
Index of Biblical Characters 129
Index of Biblical Quotations and References 131

Preface

This is a book I have wanted to write for quite some time now. But while the basic content has been more or less readily at hand there has been the problem of putting it together in a manner untrammeled by certain aspects of my academic background which I have particularly sought to free the material from.

The clue to solving that problem came in reading the conclusion to Chaucer's 'Nun's Priest's Tale', where the priest 'legitimises' the bawdy content of his tale in the following way:

> But ye that holden this tale a folye
> As of a fox, or of a cok and hen,
> Taketh the moralitee, good men.
> For seint Paul seith, that al that writen is,
> To our doctryne it is y-write, y-wis.
> Taketh the fruyt, and lat the chaf be stille.

This book does not tell an imaginary tale, nor does its content need to be legitimised or excused. But it is about 'coks' and 'hens' and the representation of gender and gender relations; St Paul is a significant contributor to its content; it does have a 'moralitee' or message; and it is written 'to our doctryne' in that its purpose is to promote discussion and learning. Nevertheless, it is not necessarily incumbent on me to point the particular moral nor to direct the teaching towards specific ends; and I have chosen quite deliberately not to do those things nor to relate the content directly to the numerous theoretic and practical contexts with which it is obviously closely connected.

In learning from the nun's priest I too have tried simply to turn over a field of some controversy while not hiding my feelings or viewpoint towards it; and then to leave it for others to take up what they find to be fruitful and to pursue that in whatever directions they will.

1 Introduction and Explanations

THE PURPOSE

This book is concerned to *display* what the bible has to say, mainly explicitly but also implicitly, about women: about their place in society as well as in the general order of things; about the way they should be treated; and about their specifically feminine characteristics. It might seem, therefore, that little else needs to be done other than to lay out, perhaps thematically, those passages in the bible that refer to such things.

To do only that, however, would ultimately be far from satisfactory; if for no other reason than that to present such a display, unheralded and unaccounted for, might suggest that what has been laid out has pretensions towards neutrality, objectivity and definitiveness — whereas what in fact does follow here has pretensions to none of those things.

It is impossible, both here or anywhere else, to lay out a completely neutral, objective, or definitive display of anything. There must, at the very least, be selection of that which is to be displayed, which in turn implies that there are reasons and purposes behind the inclusion of material which turns up as well as the exclusion of that which does not. There is no such thing as an innocent reading of anything; and the reading of the bible which has led to the following selections being chosen for display has been anything but innocent. I have had a case to make out; and consequently that which is displayed tends to support this case.

It does not do so unfairly, however. Neutrality, objectivity, and even innocence are matters of degree in such things, and I have leant in their direction just about as far as I have found it possible given both the source material at hand, and the context in which and for which it is to be displayed. For instance, extremely little has been deliberately omitted, things unsympathetic to my case have not been merely ignored or uncaringly passed over, and quotations have not been tortured out of context to make the point I want them to make. And yet it is still not completely neutral or innocent; and so in order to give it the greatest credence possible it becomes incumbent upon me to make explicit why the display has been arranged, how it has been arranged, what it is meant to demonstrate, and what claims to justification might underlie all of this. At the very least there needs to be spelled out somewhere why it was that the bible of all things was chosen as the object for this exercise; what I have taken the bible to be and to include; what text I have chosen; how I have approached and interpreted the bible for the purpose of this exercise; and just what particular exercise was being undertaken anyway, and why it was being undertaken. The last can be spelt out first; after which we can look more closely in the direction of the bible.

The real subject of this book is women, and representations of women. Now it is no secret that women in Judeo-Christian societies have been, since the beginning of recorded history and up to and including the very recent past if not the actual present, second class citizens. This state of affairs is not, of course, unique to Judeo-Christian societies. In certain other societies women have far fewer rights, freedoms and options; and within Judeo-Christian societies things used to be a great deal more unfavourable for women than they are now. As the glittering advertisements and the pop songs keep telling us, women within Judeo-Christian societies have come a long way indeed. What the advertisements and the songs usually fail to mention, however, is that women have had to struggle for everything they have got (and that usually they have had to struggle more than men to get any particular thing), that what women have got they usually got well after men had had it, and that there still remains a multitude of things available to men (those seemingly endless 'last' bastions of male prerogative) which are as yet unavailable to women. And even where there are declarations of availability or supposedly equal opportunity, reality often reveals marked unavailability and vast inequalities based on a supposed qualitative gender difference, itself often reflected or expressed in common pejorative prejudicial attitudes to women. The blunt fact of the matter is that, in general, women are thought of and treated not just differently from men but as worse than men — as inferior to men, as having fewer rights than men, and quite commonly as bearers of certain distasteful traits and qualities supposedly predominant in if not unique to the female of the species.

This much would be difficult to deny. But why is this the case: why have our prevailing attitudes and practices towards women been as they were, and why do they remain in the forms in which they are manifested today?

These questions need to be answered, and answered comprehensively; and a beginning has been made along many directions and in many different areas. This particular book aims to make a modest contribution towards answering those questions by presenting what it is hoped will be a plausible case that the bible has had a large part to play in fostering particular perceptions of women in an influential way over a long period of time.

WHY THE BIBLE?

The bible has been chosen on the *assumption* that it, more than anything else, has influenced and directed the perceptions and ways of thinking of the Judeo-Christian world in general for at least the last two thousand years — with its widest and deepest influence coming in the last five hundred years — and that it, more than anything, still influences and directs the perceptions and ways of thinking in today's Judeo-Christian world in general even though it is no longer studied or followed through compulsion or under pain of death.

It cannot be emphasised too much, however, that the basic assumption as outlined above is nothing more than an assumption and must continue to remain an assumption; mainly because influence, especially in the realm of beliefs and perceptions, is notoriously difficult if not impossible to pin down let alone quantify. Even when people openly admit or declare that certain things have (or have not) significantly influenced their thought they can easily be wrong; and historians and pseudo-historians who unabashedly and unashamedly chart out 'progressions' or developments in thought and practice in terms of causal influential chains are far more at risk than they usually take care to acknowledge. To say that anything or anyone influenced anyone else's thinking, either positively or negatively, is problematic; while to attempt to locate, fix or quantify such influence tends towards pure folly. In the absence of a certain sort of empirical evidence (which is almost always absent) the best one can hope for when dealing with influence is to lay out conditions whereby such influence might occur and show that these conditions existed in the case under consideration. And in attempting to show further that something was (or is) a *major* influence on something else one can do little more than indicate that, in the particular case under consideration these conditions can be shown to have prevailed in a most propitious manner.

Now the particular issue of the influence of the bible on perception is one in which much of the relevant and useful sorts of empirical evidence required is, by and large, both missing and beyond location, and so it can not really be proved that the bible has been the major influence in directing and forming particular or general ways of thought within the

Judeo-Christian world. We can, however, make out a plausible case that the bible was (and is) well placed to so direct and form thought; and that it was (and is) better placed to do this than other potential sources of influence; and to this end the four conditions on which such a case is being based shall now be laid out. (It can be added, less than modestly this time that regardless of how convincing or otherwise this case may be, the following two major parts of this book still make interesting reading.)

(a) The time factor
The bible has been around for a long time. Much of the Old Testament (hereafter OT) dates back over three thousand years in some known written form or another (even given that parts were at times preserved by oral tradition), while the youngest part of the OT is known to have existed in written form since the second century BC. A complete Hebrew version is known to have existed from the second century AD onwards, and Hebrew manuscripts from the ninth century AD onwards still survive today. A Greek version was known of as far back as the third century BC; and a Latin version appeared coincidentally with the earliest spread of Christianity. The New Testament (hereafter NT) was originally written in Greek. Manuscripts of the 'complete' bible[1] date from as far back as the middle of the fourth century AD: and by the end of that century Jerome had produced a newer Latin version, the Vulgate. Various fragments of the bible were translated into English at odd and varying times before a complete English translation (the Wycliffe) appeared in 1382. A Latin version of the bible became the first book produced by the process of movable-type printing; and in 1611 a version was prepared for James I of England which, since its publication, has been known and used by English speaking protestants as the Authorised Version (hereafter AV). A revised version was published in 1881, the American Standard Version appeared in 1901, and the New English Bible (hereafter NEB) was published in 1961 (OT) and 1970

(NT): 1970 also saw the publication of the New American Bible designed to replace the Douay Version – that generally used by English speaking Roman Catholics and which incorporates additional books from the Apocrypha within the OT. Today the whole of the bible can be found translated into over two hundred languages, while particular varying parts have been translated into a further thousand languages.

Clearly little, if anything, has been around as long, and at the same time been as continuously available to the literate sections of Judeo-Christian communities, as the bible. And these literate sections, by reading and speaking the bible, as well as in many other ways, have ensured that it has also been available to the non-literate sections as well. But this alone is by no means sufficient to establish a special case for the bible concerning its potential to influence past and contemporary perceptions, and so other factors must also be considered.

(b) The saturation factor
The Upanishads, and the works of Plato and Aristotle, have existed for much the same period of time as the bible, but have not been continuously available within Judeo-Christian societies; although Plato and Aristotle have been continuously available to the post-mediaeval English-speaking world. The works of Homer, Aeschylus, Sophocles and Euripides have also been around for as long as even the oldest sections of the bible, and at the same time they have maintained a large measure of continuous availability. One thing which distinguishes the bible, however, from these and all other long-surviving works is not just the greater continuity of availability but also the actual *degree* of availability. Put bluntly, the bible has been far more commonly and readily 'available' over the past two thousand years than any other book or piece of literature: in fact so much so that our socio-cultural milieu is saturated with it. Three matters need to be considered in relation to this.

First; in terms of sheer quantity the bible wins hands down. It is the most widely printed and distributed book in history by a long, long way; and more people have owned (or have had immediate access to) a bible than any other book whatsoever. It does not, of course, necessarily follow that all those possessing or having immediate access to a copy of the bible actually read it; but it would, nevertheless, be fairly safe to assume that the bible has been the most widely read book if not in the whole of history then certainly in the Judeo-Christian world.

Second; the bible has commonly held a very special place among books. If a house possessed only one book, that book was most likely to be the bible; if a house possessed many books the bible was the one most likely to be among them; and if any book was read from on a regular daily basis that book was sure to be the bible. Further, the bible was once to be found (mainly due to the efforts of the Gideons) in every hotel room, as well as in military quarters, hospitals and prisons. Excerpts from the bible are printed daily in the popular press, a number of radio and TV spots are also devoted to it each day, and in many large cities one can simply dial the telephone and hear in return a recorded reading from the bible. Nothing like the same could ever be said for Plato's *Republic*, Tolstoy's *War and Peace*, or even so popular a 'classic' as *Robinson Crusoe*.

Third; the bible is, and has been 'available' in a multitude of forms in addition to its common book form. Much of it can be 'read', even by the illiterate, in the carvings and glass art of Chartres Cathedral, and to a lesser extent in many other major places of worship. The bible has also been an extremely fertile source for the visual arts, and allusions to and from it permeate all aspects of our literature. Thus even though one might not have direct contact with the printed bible *per se*, it would be extremely difficult in the course of leading a normal life, either today or in the past, not to continually encounter things which derive directly and indirectly from such contact. The bible permeates just about every aspect of our way of life; for example our code of behaviour, our rituals and mores, a large amount of our law, and even the very routine of the passage of our time (punctuated as it is by sabbatical rest days, and Easter, Christmas, Yom Kippur and Pesach); and it does this to a far greater degree than any other potential source of influence. In fact it is only because such a state of saturation does exist that we can refer meaningfully to a society or a historical epoch as being Jewish, or Christian, or Judeo-Christian in the first place. And yet significant though this is, it is by no means the end of it; the bible has yet another major claim to distinction.

(c) The inspirational factor
Theologians might disagree among themselves with regard to which specific books should be included in the bible, but they are largely in agreement over the criteria whereby a book is judged as deserving of such a place. The biblical books, or the canon, are regarded (and declared) as bearing a special authority; they are considered to be divinely inspired. The books themselves have human authors of course; they use the changing and imperfect language of the world; and they have suffered endless translation, reappraisal and copying. Thus the stamp of mortal hands is upon them; and yet their text, their message, and their substance is allegedly directly inspired by God and so bears divine authority. In this most significant of ways, then, do the words of Job, Samuel and Paul differ from those of Plato, Descartes and Rousseau; just as in the same way the laws laid down in Leviticus, Deuteronomy and Matthew differ from those laid down by social legislating bodies. In each case the former are directly linked with divine authority, while the latter can at best claim only an indirect link and at worst be accused of having no link whatsoever. This all places the bible in a very special position indeed.

Consider, for example, the views expressed by Rousseau towards women in Book V of *Emile*; and the views expressed by Paul regarding women as found in his epistles to the Corinthians, the Ephesians, the Colossians, and to Timothy. What Rousseau says can be taken or left, concurred with or cast aside as the arrogant expression of eighteenth-century male chauvinism. So too can Paul's words be taken or left: but they cannot be so easily cast aside as the expression of first-century Roman-flavoured misogynism if the twenty-seven books of the NT, of which Paul's epistles make up fourteen, are regarded as being inspired and bearing God's authority. If this much is taken seriously then Paul's words and views, so similar to Rousseau's, take on a very particular backing and a special kind of authority, which might not be recognised by some people, but which nevertheless cannot be superseded by any higher form of authority within the *Weltanschauung* in which they are generated and which they help to sustain. The overall result is that Paul's statements become especially difficult to argue with, let alone refute; and it can even follow that works such as Book V of Rousseau's *Emile* might be regarded by some as a worthwhile lay expression of what had already been sealed by divine authority. Similarly, Paul said 'Let your women keep silent in the churches: for it is not permitted unto them to speak...'; and for two thousand years now women have been kept from speaking and officiating in orthodox Christian churches by those who directly and openly seek justification for their position in the claim that Paul's pronouncement was divinely inspired and bears God's authority.[2]

For a second example consider the difficulties homosexuals have faced over the past two thousand years; and the difficulties they still face today, in having law and public opinion liberalised in their direction. It appears as though, no matter what barriers are broken down and no matter what changes are made, one stumbling block still remains. It is written, and regularly quoted against homosexuals, that:

> If a man also lieth with mankind, as he lieth with a woman, both of them have committed an abomination...

Unfortunately, for the homosexuals, these words have been written in the bible (Leviticus 20:13): they would surely count far less if they came from Aristotle or Hippocrates or some other mere mortal and thus did not presume or have presumed upon them the backing of divine authority.

None of the above, however, is meant to suggest that these days everybody believes in the divine inspiration and authority of the bible. Far from it. But it is not necessary for everyone to be a believer for the point about the bible's special status to hold. The belief needs only to be a historically established tenable option (and in this particular case it is also one which is incapable of being disproved). The bible lays claim to divine inspiration; many sane, intelligent, rational people have held and argued that it is divinely inspired; and there is no way to disprove such a claim — thus the possibility exists that it might be what is claimed for it and so deserve its special authority and status. We tend not to regard the complete works of Shakespeare, the *Iliad*, or anything else in our literature in quite the same way.

A particular historical instance can illustrate here the point about the very special status of the biblical word which in times past, as well as in times present, has sufficed as the arbiter in any number of disputes, decisions and definitions. Consider, then, what might, for want of a better name, be known as 'The Witches' Circle'.

It is written in Exodus 22:18 that: 'Thou shalt not suffer a witch to live.' Presumably, then, one can and ought to kill any witch one finds. A major problem, however, at least in seventeenth-century England, was to actually recognise a witch, for as Thomas has so carefully detailed, there was little consensus or clarity in England at that time as to just what constituted a witch in the first place.[3] But here Wilson's *Complete Christian Dictionary* of 1612 came to the rescue, defining a witch as 'one that exerciseth devilish and wicked acts, such as be named in Deut. 18.10, Ex. 22.18.' What acts then, do we find named in the bible of 1611? As it turns out, not many. At Deuteronomy 18:10 it says:

> There shall not be found among you any one that maketh his

son or his daughter to pass through fire, or that useth divination, or an observer of times, or an enchanter, or a witch,

while Exodus 22:18 says as quoted above and no more: 'Thou shalt not suffer a witch to live.' Nevertheless the circle is complete: the bible passes the sentence on witches and is also set up as the arbiter of what a witch is — even though it does not tell us precisely what we need to know.

(d) The susceptibility factor
So far we have considered factors about the bible which make it well placed to influence consciousness and perception; to these can now be added a factor about people, and more particularly about their relation to and interrelation with the bible, which also serves to establish propitious conditions for the bible's role in directing and forming thought.

Basically the bible is read by two types of people: those who believe in it (i.e. who believe it is divinely inspired and ought to guide action in the world), and those who don't. Of the first group enough has been said already — they accept the bible's teaching and are susceptible to its word (regardless of how well they might put the word into practice). But what of the second group: those who take up the bible in a context of disbelief?

In the absence of sound empirical evidence a wide, but hopefully not wild generalisation can be posited — namely that many people who turn to serious reading of the bible after a period of basic disbelief or disdain do so in an attempt to fulfil a particular need at a time when other previously-trodden avenues no longer appear to be leading in a desired and desirable direction. Put another way, it is being suggested here that these people turn to the bible for guidance and direction, for prescriptions and for answers. After all, if a person wants no more than a good read, a bit of escapism or a bed-time wind-down there is more than enough around to satisfy that sort of need. And if a person wants to engage with philosophy, or fictional characters facing and coping with life's problems, or fine and complex poetry, then the works of those such as Bertrand Russell, Tolstoy and Wordsworth might be taken up. But when people go past all those alternatives, and others as well, and turn specifically to the bible, it would not be too far-fetched to suggest that in many cases they do so in a particular frame of mind which is at least conducive to assimilating and accepting what is to be found there. Conversely, by far the largest part of literature (including history and philosophy) is not didactic in the way the bible is, nor does it offer what the bible purports to offer. So, put together the way people commonly come to the bible with what the bible holds out to them in return, and it is feasible to suggest that conditions for susceptibility and impressionability would prevail in a way unlikely to be matched by human contact with any other body of literature.

*

And so, back to our central question: why the bible? In short, because it has been continuously available to us for so long, *and* because it has saturated our background consciousness so variedly and so deeply, *and* because it claims to speak through divine inspiration and with divine authority and is commonly accepted as such, *and* because it is likely that people come to it in a particular frame of mind conducive to accepting and believing what it says, it seems reasonable to contend, *when all of these things are taken together*, that the bible has been and continues to be extremely well placed to influence consciousness, perception, and the general way in which the world is seen. Further, given the bible's unrivalled longevity and availability, the very breadth and depth of its saturation in terms of which everything else runs a far distant second, its unique claims regarding divine inspiration and authority, and what is likely to be a unique and unrivalled effect upon sympathetic readers, it would seem reasonable to contend that the bible is not only well placed but rather is best placed to be the major determining theoretic influence within the Judeo-Christian world — and this even in the wake of the church's gradual loss of secular power since the sixteenth century, as well as in the shadow of increasingly powerful alternative practical and theoretical determinants which surround us today as never before.

Four closing points should now be added to make clearer just what is, and is not, being claimed.

First; it is by no means being claimed that all those who have been directly exposed to the bible come to believe all of it, or all of it with equal intensity, or even any of it, let alone that they come to act upon it consistently. It is simply being suggested that the bible is well placed, and even best placed, to influence and determine consciousness; that it has done this for a long period of time and still continues to do this; but not that it does so infallibly, inescapably, or even uniformly in terms of its own content. For instance the bible states that in order to be perfect we must sell what we have and give the proceeds to the poor (Matthew 19:21): it also states in many places that we should not commit murder. But since few people do sell up everything and give the money to the poor, whereas most people do not in fact commit murder, it is clear that directives in the bible are not followed with equal enthusiasm, nor do they necessarily lead to prompt universal action.

Second; it is not being claimed that direct exposure to the bible is necessary for its ideas to be learnt and assimilated. On the one hand, some biblical ideas have long ago passed into the realms of 'common sense' and/or socio-cultural norms and mores. On the other hand, the level of saturation which has now been achieved makes it unnecessary for anyone to have to confront the bible directly to pick up the ideas and themes included in it. Thus to argue that the bible is read less now than a century ago, even if that were correct, is not the same as arguing that the bible's influence, and its potential to influence is diminishing.

Third; it is not being claimed that people necessarily know that a biblical 'basis' exists for those beliefs they hold which actually are to be found in the bible. For instance the bible says:

> The woman shall not wear that which pertaineth unto a man, neither shall a man put on a woman's garment: for all that do so are abomination unto the LORD thy God.
>
> Deuteronomy 22:5

and yet it is more than likely that many among the vast numbers who regard transvestism as evil and sinful, as a perversion and even an abomination, would be unaware of the existence of that verse in the bible. What *is* being claimed, however, is that the above verse is well placed to influence opinion against transvestism, that it may in the past have had something to do with forming the long-standing negative and pejorative views that prevail against transvestism within our socio-cultural milieu, and that should a case against transvestism ever need to be mounted or 'clinched' it's pretty certain that that verse will be trotted out (just as Leviticus 20:13 is regularly trotted out by those Christians and Jews alike, who are outraged at the concessions being made to homosexuals these days).

Finally; it is not being claimed that everything which is found in the bible originated there. For instance the bible states (Leviticus 15:10) that a woman shall be 'put apart' from her community during her menstrual period; yet this practice is known to have existed quite widely well before the recording of Leviticus. Similarly, part of what Jesus says about first getting one's own self sorted out before correcting others (Matthew 7:3–5) was pretty much covered by Plato four centuries earlier in *The Republic*, Book VII. Obviously some of the points which are to be found in the bible may have filtered down through other channels as well; to claim that the bible is a major influence in promulgating ideas is not to claim that those ideas had to have originated in the bible (even if their appearance within the canon is the 'official' mark of their divine authority).

SOURCES, TRANSLATIONS, TEXTS AND INTERPRETATIONS

As noted earlier the bible can be found today, either in part or in whole, in well over a thousand languages. One of these languages is English, but this does not mean that there is a single English version or a universally accepted authoritative English version. Far from it. Over the past six hundred years English versions of the bible have proliferated, and different groups have settled on different versions or new revisions of particular versions as being authoritative and definitive. Which of these, however, provides the best translation from the classical Hebrew, ancient Aramaic, and early Greek, or which contains the best established collection of truly inspired books, or which captures most accurately the spirit of the earliest texts and also corrects most of the copyists' errors is not the concern of this book.

In what follows two versions of the bible have been chosen and employed — one as a primary source and the other as a secondary source — according to one criterion, and towards one end. The criterion is that of *exposure*: what has been sought out is the version that has been most contacted by most people, and this clearly is the AV of 1611 which becomes our primary source; while our secondary source is the 'officially approved' modern version looming as its successor among protestants — the NEB of 1961 and 1970. The end in question is to display sections of the text as they appear in either one or both of those two most commonly encountered versions.

In every instance bar one in what follows, the text displayed shall be that of the AV. In each and every case, however, the text of the AV has been checked against that of the NEB; but the NEB text has been displayed only in those instances where it differs, or fails to differ, from the AV in ways considered relevant to the overall thesis or theme of this book.

Actually, an important and relevant point can be taken

from an overall comparison of the two complete texts. Mostly only the language changes; occasionally there is a difference in detail (which, as we shall see, can be quite significant); but at times the changes are fairly large. For instance, in the NEB, Nehemiah 4 concludes (my italics):

> So neither I nor my kinsmen nor the men under me nor my bodyguard ever took off our clothes, *each keeping his right hand* on his weapon

and a footnote indicates the italicised section as 'probable' since the Hebrew is obscure. However, in the AV it comes out, and has come out since 1611, in Nehemiah 4:23 as:

> So neither I, nor my brethren, nor my servants, nor the men of the guard which followed me, none of us put off our clothes, saving that every one put them off for washing.

We might ask where the compilers of the AV got that bit about washing, and why they stuck it in; even though the specific matter is of very little importance. The general principle, however, is of very great concern; for often things appear in the AV which have been shown by later scholars to have little justification for inclusion, and which in many cases, but not all, disappear from later revisions. And as far as the theme of this book is concerned there are quite a few relevant sections to be found.

For instance; in many places in Leviticus, chapters 15 to 20 inclusive, the AV refers to menstruating women as 'having their sickness' and being 'unclean', whereas in the NEB all references to 'sickness' have been removed yet references to 'uncleanliness' remain. In Judges 19:1–9 there is the story of a Levite who goes to Bethlehem to fetch home his wife who, in the AV, 'played the whore against him, and went away from him unto her father's house'; but who, in the NEB, had left him merely in 'a fit of anger'. And in I Corinthians 6:9–10 Paul lists those who will not inherit the kingdom of God —

in the AV the list goes like this:

> ...neither fornicators, nor idolaters, nor adulterers, nor effeminate, nor abusers of themselves with mankind,
> Nor thieves, nor covetous, nor drunkards, nor revilers, nor extortioners shall inherit the kingdom of God.

whereas in the NEB the list is identical except that the 'effeminate' have been left out. (Actually it is more the case that in the AV the effeminate, along with the notion that the Levite's wife had played the whore, have been rather unjustifiably *slipped in*, as has the notion that menstruation is a 'sickness'.)

Now it is by no means our purpose here to continue to arbitrate on such differences, let alone to attempt to resolve them. It is important, however, that they are at least pointed out; not just because of the horrendous problems they cause fundamentalists or anyone who quotes the bible for political and/or moral purposes (what if the original Leviticus were found tomorrow and was seen to contain no condemnation of homosexuality at 20:13?), and not just because they explain historical oddities such as Michelangelo portraying Moses with horns emanating from his forehead through following Jerome's mis-translation of 'light' in the Vulgate, but rather because for most people in most cases the words of the AV especially are taken (and presented) as if they were largely if not entirely unproblematic. It may not be desirable but it is nevertheless the case that almost everybody who reads the bible reads it neither critically nor historically nor theologically, but *literally*. And in so reading the AV over the last three hundred and seventy or so years people have encountered, and still encounter, those points noted above; namely particular disparaging comments about women, an attack and a negative judgment passed upon those with effeminate characteristics, and a continuing association of menstruation with sickness — notions which surely must have had their effect in the formulation of laws, customs, beliefs and mores over that period of time; and yet notions whose place in the original inspiration have now been shown by certain modern scholars employing more careful collaborative and informed research and examination of the ancient texts, to be extremely tenuous and dubious.

Let all that be as it may, however; for what counts most in considering the possible influence the bible may have had in forming consciousness and beliefs are the words that actually constitute the text, and not why they have been chosen or what their actual standing with regard to originality and authenticity might be. And it is largely for this reason that in what follows here there shall be no attempt at analysis of the chosen primary text, no concern with assessing its adequacy as a translation, no parade of explanations or alternative readings or interpretations, and not even an indication of what are now very clearly recognised — by theologians, linguists, and historians — to be errors. The text shall simply be laid out to be read in the way most people have read it throughout history and still read it today — literally.

This position is perfectly reasonable and defensible. The vast majority of people who read Leviticus 20:18 (and elsewhere) of a menstruating woman as 'having her sickness' are surely unaware as to whether theologians doubt the authenticity of this verse or not; whether 'sickness' is or is not an adequate translation from the original; or even of the range of nuances of meaning that 'sickness' had in 1611. All of these things are matters of esoteric investigation, undertaken by very few: they are simply not on the agenda of almost everyone who has read and/or quoted the AV over the last three hundred and seventy years — and thus they shall not be on the agenda here either. The one thing we can be quite certain of is that readers of and listeners to the AV have found menstruation continually associated with sickness and uncleanliness. We know that the AV did not originate this association, and also that in the past four centuries it could easily have been encountered elsewhere — but the association is there, and we can at least presume, especially given the argument of the previous section, that at some time or another and in some cases it has stuck. Certainly even today there is still widespread suspicion, secrecy and even fear surrounding menstruation, and it is still commonly regarded as a state of uncleanliness.[4] We can reasonably presume that the bible, simply through literal display, has had its part to play in forming and perpetuating such attitudes.

To conclude, then: the two following chapters of this book will be concerned centrally with textual display (of the AV) and not with matters of theology, linguistics or history. Further; the textual displays will usually be presented with only as much surrounding context as is necessary to reinforce or place the actual text being displayed. This is not being done only in the interests of economy, however. The method also replicates the way in which biblical text is usually presented to (and commonly studied by) people — namely in a literal piecemeal fashion whereby a line or two or a verse or a couple of verses, either read, written out or in these days emblazoned across a placard, either 'speaks for itself' or forms the basis for a more elaborate sermon or lesson.

ON SELECTION

Careful selection from the bible can go a long way towards supporting or demonstrating virtually anything. Take for instance the quaint little myth that an old grey-haired person is virtuous and wise: 'justification' can be found in the bible:

> The hoary head is a crown of glory, if it be found in the way of righteousness.
> [NEB — Grey hair is a crown of glory and is won by a virtuous life.]
>   Proverbs 16:31.

Similarly we can find 'support' for the still common idea that being right-handed is normal or at least better than being left-handed (less than thirty years ago schools were actually converting left-handed writers into right-handers) in biblical phrases which link the right side of the body with good and the left side with evil and foolishness. For instance:

> A wise man's heart is at his right hand; but a fool's heart at his left.
> [NEB — The mind of the wise man faces right, but the mind of the fool faces left.]
>
> Ecclesiastes 10:2.

And the bible even suggests that it's wrong for a man to wear his hair long:

> Doth not even nature itself teach you, that, if a man have long hair, it is a shame unto him?
>
> I Corinthians 11:14

It is not really difficult to find an occasional or isolated verse in the bible which can appear, at least on the face of it, to support just about any position one wants to hold or put forward. There is a sting in the tail of this, however, for by the same token it becomes equally easy to find some other verse which, again on the face of it, appears to contradict the position previously taken (which is hardly surprising given the diversity of sources, in both time and space, which make up the canon). For example, the bible also has something favourable to say about men having long hair — and thus uncut male locks are not always depicted as shameful:

> And the LORD spake unto Moses, saying
> ... When either man or woman shall separate themselves to vow a vow of a Nazarite, to separate themselves unto the LORD...
> All the days of the vow of his separation there shall no razor come upon his head ... he shall be holy, and shall let the locks of the hair of his head grow.
>
> Numbers 6:1–5

Introduction and Explanations

The mighty Samson was such a Nazarite (and his might was in his long hair):

> ... There hath not come a razor upon mine head; for I have been a Nazarite unto God from my mother's womb: if I be shaven, then my strength will go from me, and I shall become weak, and be like any other man.
>
> Judges 16:17

and Jesus Christ himself is commonly pictured *outside of the bible* as having long hair presumably because, as a citizen of Nazareth, he too was a Nazarite, albeit of a different sort.

There are some among those who have great knowledge of the bible who enjoy playing such a game of point-counterpoint. They can play it with isolated examples regarding trivial issues (as above) or they can play it in a far more sustained way with other particular issues of much greater import. Consider, for instance, the matter of giving charity to the poor. By means of selective quoting it would be possible to fill a small volume with verses exhorting the rich and the not so rich to give to the poor; but at the same time it is also possible to fill a similar volume with verses warning against being generous, or too generous towards the poor, and even suggesting the futility and inadvisability of helping the poor since they are allegedly part of God's design. In similar vein one could fill a significantly thicker volume with verses which urge people to rise up and act in this world against injustice and oppression; but then go on to match this with an equally-thick volume of verses suggesting either that we meekly bear our burden in this world since the real rewards are in the next one, and/or that those who put up with it all meekly will inherit this world as well. And it is not merely a matter of playing point-counterpoint, of course: by judicious selection of quotations it is easy to build up substantial cases for men either having long hair or short hair, for being charitable towards the poor or leaving them to their own devices, and for taking up arms against a sea of troubles or for meekly suffering the slings and arrows of outrageous fortune.

What the bible might advise us to do in any particular circumstances, then, could come down to which bits are selectively quoted — and for those people who are not closely conversant with the whole bible it often does come down to precisely that: to the particular sections which are pointed out and highlighted. How the bible has actually been used in history in order to influence action and perception in particular directions at particular times has regrettably been left poorly charted and is extremely difficult if not impossible to pin down, but records do occasionally remain and oral history tends to offer some insights. For instance, it is well known that chaplains at the front in the second world war read passages to the soldiers relating to the need (even the holy mission) of taking up a sword against injustice, and of the glories of everlasting salvation for those who died in the process, and conveniently overlooked those passages about turning the other cheek. It is also well documented that, amid the declining social conditions in Welsh mining villages a century or so ago the clergy notoriously based their sermons and lessons on key biblical passages advocating passivity and stoicism in the face of adversity. Conversely, some clergy in today's third world have become renowned for pointing out to the peasants those passages which urge the oppressed to rise up against their oppressors. When women mobilise in order to gain more power and to break down gender discrimination they are commonly known to do so behind banners bearing the text from Galatians 3:28; when men try to keep them from infiltrating the clergy they in turn hold up I Corinthians 14:34–35 and I Timothy 2:11–12. And there is one favourite chestnut which is quoted and paraphrased time and time again when it is felt that people need to be reminded about the source of authority and why it must be obeyed:

> Let every soul be subject unto the higher powers. For there is no power but of God: the powers that be are ordained of God.

Introduction and Explanations

> Whosoever therefore resisteth the power, resisteth the ordinance of God: and they that resist shall receive to themselves damnation.
> For rulers are not a terror to good works, but to the evil. Wilt thou then not be afraid of the power? do that which is good, and thou shalt have praise of the same:
> For he is the minister of God to thee for good. But if thou do that which is evil, be afraid; for he beareth not the sword in vain: for he is the minister of God, a revenger to execute wrath upon him that doeth evil.
> Wherefore ye must needs be subject, not only for wrath, but also for conscience sake.
> For this cause pay ye tribute also: for they are God's ministers, attending continually upon this very thing.
>
> Romans 13:1–6

Prince Charles used this one when explaining to the people of Papua-New Guinea (many of them illiterate natives) what self-rule was all about at the official declaration of independence of that country: interestingly it does not seem to have been bandied around much concerning Idi Amin or Pol Pot.[5]

But now to the particular point at issue. The quotations on which the following two chapters of this book are based are, of course, selective. They are not, however, unfairly or outrageously so. There are some passages in the bible which tend towards the opposite case from that being presented here, and usually (but not always) these have been left out. But there are not many of them. Unlike the 'charity' issue or the 'action/passivity' debate an equally large number of instances do not stack up on either side. In what follows here passages have been sought out which depict women in certain ways, and this has been done unashamedly in terms of a two-handed 'justification'. On the one hand the bible is simply being used in the way that it is so commonly used by others — to put forward specific and definitive points. But on the other hand (and this is of great importance) while the selections which follow are, in a sense disproportionate, they come from an area where massive disproportion already exists in the bible. A partially blind eye has at times been turned towards statements regarding certain qualities of women such as those highlighted, for instance, in the stories of Ruth and Naomi, but the passages that have been passed over are rare exceptions (and ones which, at least with Ruth, could have been turned to other purposes anyway); and little mention has been made of Mary, mother of Christ — but then again there is very little mention of her in the bible itself: in the whole of the NT only Luke's Gospel takes serious, and yet still brief notice of her. It is more the case that the passages and attitudes to be displayed in what follows here, while being quite selective, *are still very much the norm* as far as the bible as a whole is concerned. Although some things have, of course, been left out, the game of point-counterpoint could not be played successfully here; and what has been selected for display could neither be matched passage for passage or claim for claim, nor even be significantly alluded against.

ON THE HISTORICAL CONTEXT

The basis of the bible might be divine authority, but the recording, preservation and transmission of this is very much a human affair; and such things, along with translations and revisions, do not take place within a vacuum but rather within very specific socio-historical contexts. This virtually self-evident point, however, raises rather tricky problems concerning the status of the biblical text and its pronouncements and prescriptions. Two central problems to confront any serious study of or concern with the bible are how much and what parts of it are divinely inspired (and conversely which parts reflect the socio-historic circumstances of the recorder or translator); and following on from this, which parts are meant to be relevant for all times and places, and which really represent the concerns, predilections and interests of some particular time and place or even some particular recorders and translators? For instance, is it possible that the commandment not to commit murder is divinely inspired and universally applicable, whereas the prescription not to eat shellfish was merely a wise precaution inserted by someone concerned with food poisoning in days that lacked refrigeration and modern hygienic controls? Or, is it not only possible but also extremely likely that human recorders of a divine inspiration related to menstruation would, in an age when menstruating women were separated out into special huts, automatically use language associated with separation and thus 'accidentally' make it appear that such separation was endorsed universally by divine authority?

There are two opposing extreme positions which can be taken on such issues. On the one hand it is often argued that the bible is human history pure and simple, to be regarded and modified as each successive age sees fit. On the other hand it is argued that the word is from God; every single little bit of it. Both of these extreme positions are rejected here: the former because it removes the inspirational factor and thus makes the bible far less of a special case regarding authority and influence; and the latter because, as we have seen already and as any serious study would continue to show us, the word changes from version to version, and the definitive divine text has at least yet to be found.

The position I am adopting here lies somewhere between the two extremes. For the purpose of the exercise the possibility of a *basis* of divine inspiration and authority is not being questioned, while at the same time it is being recognised that such a basis would necessarily have to be filtered and transmitted through human socio-cultural and historic contexts. The actual word might have been revealed directly or even metaphorically; but when humans came to record it they had little option but to use the language, the reference points (e.g. the names of once-locally-growing trees), the attitudes, the preconceptions, their existing beliefs and so on as the context in which to insert and transcribe the divine inspiration they received — with each subsequent translator or reviser doing much the same thing.

This much, however, does not resolve anything regarding specific matters of textual authenticity and/or inspiration, and it is by no means my purpose in this book to attempt to arbitrate on such questions. But while the stance being taken here doesn't actually resolve specific problems (such as whether the death penalty imposed in Leviticus 20:12 really is as God wants it, and wants it for all times and places) it does clarify and help justify a more general position regarding the biblical word. If the possibility of divine inspiration is allowed in the first place, then historical considerations are revealed as, at best, important and necessary but never as sufficient; and within this sort of context no part of the bible can be accepted or excused on historical grounds alone, nor can any part be dismissed only on such grounds other than by showing that the part in question is undeniably a later non-inspired insertion (as the AV reference to the effeminate in I Corinthians 6:9 appears to be). We can now make the overall point we seek in relation to the actual topic of this book — the bible's representation of women.

The bible was originally written down over a long historical period in which men were continually warring while women wept, kept the tent, and looked after the children. It was a period when women had few rights, and during which they were given away or sold, into either marriage or slavery, like chattels. It is therefore not surprising that the biblical text reflects and speaks the language of such practices and attitudes, and that it is peppered with statements such as 'thy desire shall be to thy husband, and he shall rule over thee' (Genesis 3:16) which, if nothing else, reflect the patriarchy of the times and represent the sort of things it would be expected that the males who recorded the bible and kept it alive orally would say. But the bible does more than merely reflect and perpetuate prevailing attitudes and practices; and it is commonplace to recognise that, as far as women and their rights (along with many other things) are concerned, the bible represents a radical advance on much of what had gone before as well as on much of what was otherwise being practised contemporaneously (even if it does seem to fall short of the ideals some people would seek today). But, in the context of the standpoint being taken here, what the bible says about women cannot be put aside as if it were meant to be applicable only to another time and place; nor can it be excused, praised, tolerated, justified or merely explained away strictly on historical grounds. To recognise that a socio-historic background and context permeates the text of the bible is to begin to become aware of a whole range of problems that surround the biblical text — it is by no means, as some would have it, to answer or account for those problems.

In the following two chapters of this book, the text of the bible shall be presented just as it stands, with extremely little if any declared concern with or interest in the historical background from which the text derives. This procedure recognises, but does not get unnecessarily bogged down in, certain problems that might otherwise be reasonably attended to; it preserves and emphasises, or at the least does not attack, the element of divine authority allegedly present in the biblical writings — the element above all others which can distinguish the bible from the total remainder of our literary heritage; and once again it mirrors or replicates the way in which biblical text is most commonly presented to and encountered by people — literally; and so in an a-historic fashion whereby a small portion might be extracted for its content, and where that content is then subjected to elaboration for didactic purposes.[6]

THE TWO TESTAMENTS

In what follows there are far more references to the OT than there are to the NT. This does not mean, however, that the NT is kinder or better disposed to women than the OT is.

The fact is rather that there is very little if any change of attitude expressed at all. The NT is simply shorter than the OT: on a *pro rata* basis the amount of text displayed from each is very near to equal, although it was not contrived to be so.

The Judeo side of the Judeo-Christian tradition does not, of course, accept the NT as inspired, and regards Christ as a historical figure rather than as the son of God. If Jews (or anyone) reading this book want to cross out all the quotations from the NT they will still find that every section bar one holds, and that the overall case loses something in volume but little in significance.

The Christian side of the Judeo-Christian tradition accepts the OT as inspired but incomplete, and also as being in need of slight modification. Christ says:

> Think not that I am come to destroy the law, or the prophets: I am not come to destroy but to fulfil.
> For verily I say unto you, Till heaven and earth pass, one jot or one tittle shall in no wise pass from the law, till all be fulfilled.[7]
> Matthew 5:17–18

but nevertheless he makes a few extensions (e.g. Matthew 5:27–8), modifications (e.g. Matthew 5:21–2), and changes (e.g. Matthew 5:33–6). However, even though all Christians do not see the need to follow all the minute laws in the OT, it is unlikely that Christians *qua* Christians could find good relevant reasons of a canonical sort for challenging the authenticity and applicability of any of the OT quotations that follow in this work.[8]

CONCLUDING POINTS

In the AV there is a large amount of italicisation in the text. For reasons of expediency, and in order to make it easier to emphasise certain things myself, I have reduced all the AV text to normal print. All italicised emphases that appear anywhere in this book, including those within passages quoted from the AV, are mine.

Finally, non-sexist language has been employed throughout this book except in direct quotations; and the convention of referring to God as a capitalised male has not been followed in the text.

2 The Place of Women

INTRODUCTION

It is written that:

> There is neither Jew nor Greek, there is neither bond nor free, there is neither male nor female: for ye are all one in Christ Jesus.
>
> Galatians 3:28

Male and female, however, are by no means depicted as one in the bible, either in the sense that 'one' might mean 'equal in standing', or in the sense of being similar in nature and character. It is rather the case that women are portrayed in the bible quite consistently as appendages of men; as possessions of men; as goods which may be sold, disposed of, given away, traded, or just ordered about by men;[1] as things which might better be seen but not heard; and even as things which, in particular situations, are better not even seen. From Genesis onwards — that is, right from the very beginning — women are to be found in secondary positions with regard to men; and this relationship of inferiority is not merely displayed but is also argued for repeatedly in the latter half of the NT. But even the display itself is significant; for right through the bible women are found (where they are found at all) bearing and raising children and keeping the tent while men fill the positions of authority and ownership and partake in battles and conquests. Women are also seen as the recipients of what could be called the rough end of a system of laws and customs which differ significantly and often in their application according to gender; at times as little more than mere offerings or sacrifices in circumstances where men are to be protected; and finally in a position of such demeaning relative consequence that the disgrace of having been killed in battle by one of them is considered to be worse than death itself.

THE ABSENCE OF WOMEN

The bible is a book (or rather, a collection of books) which is very heavily male dominated. The original inspiration and recording seems to have taken place largely if not entirely through and by men. Many books are directly attributed to men in their titles; others, such as the Pentateuch (or the five books of Moses) are very commonly, and if anything only marginally less directly, ascribed to men; all the prophets, who contribute fifteen books to the OT, are male; the four versions of the Gospel in the NT are each the work of men; the authors of all twenty-one NT epistles are men; and the two remaining books of the NT, namely Acts and Revelation, were also written by men. In fact only two of the sixty-six books in the AV and NEB canon bear women's names in their titles; and while the content of these books has more to do with women than is usually found elsewhere, the women in question (Ruth and Esther) are not generally considered to be the original authors of the books, and the books themselves are extremely short, together comprising only fourteen chapters in the AV and overall far less than one per cent of the total canon.

But it is not only in the original inspiration and authorship that women are significantly absent. The bible has been, in part or whole, recorded, committed to memory and oral transmission, and consistently revised and translated for over two thousand years, with such labours falling largely on the shoulders of men. The seventy-two people who produced the Septuagint more than two thousand years ago were all men, as were the members of the AD 382 Council which officially established the canon of the NT: famous individual translations such as those of Jerome, Bede, Wycliffe and Erasmus are not interspersed with female names; and the large groups of scholars, translators and literary advisers who worked to produce the AV and the NEB were significantly (and in the latter case embarrassingly) devoid — or at best, very short — of women. Thus we see that it has been almost exclusively 'men only' with regard to receiving the original inspiration, as well as recording and translating, and thus preserving and presenting its content.

Given this historical circumstance it is not surprising that the actual content of the bible is itself very largely male oriented and male dominated; that it is primarily the story of men and largely a record of the sorts of socio-historic events which men have come to dominate and direct.

The sixty-six books of the bible make up a vast chronicle which abounds with characters ranging from the very famous like Moses, Solomon and Christ, down to seemingly endless lists of largely forgotten folk who begat other largely forgotten folk as the drama unfolds and develops from the very creation itself, through the beginnings of 'civilisation as we know it', into the earliest days of the Christian era and up until the revelation of John. Very few of the main characters in the saga, as recorded, are women. Genesis, for instance, in charting the massive sweep from the creation of the universe to the relatively recent death of Joseph in Egypt,[2] introduces us to a large number of men, many of whom, like Adam, Cain, Abel, Enoch, Noah, Shem, Ham, Japeth, Abraham, Lot, Isaac, Esau, Jacob and Joseph are quite well known; and yet is unusually quiet about the women who must at least have done their share in all the begetting which moved things forward from the primeval setting of the sixth day to the time of the impending bondage of the Hebrews within a refined and well developed Egyptian civilisation.

The women in Genesis, and this holds true for the whole of the bible, can be divided roughly into five quite clearly recognisable groups.

In the first place there are those very famous women who, although extremely well known, are never actually named but instead are defined and described only in terms of their relationship to a male. Highly prominent among this group are Noah's wife, Lot's wife, and the wives of Noah's sons — Shem, Ham and Japeth. It is of considerable interest that in the whole saga of the flood and the ark (Genesis 6–9) Noah and his sons are continually named, but the identities of the only four people saved with them out of the first period of human existence — that is, the grandmother and the three mothers of the whole human race to follow — were neither recorded nor considered in their own right. Regardless of who these women were or what they did, it was considered sufficient to recognise them only in terms of the relationship they bore to their husbands. And the case of Lot's wife is extremely similar. She plays virtually no part in his history — in fact only once (Genesis 19:15) are we even made aware that Lot has a wife — until that almost gratuitous instant, of which more shall be said later, (Genesis 19:26) in which she disobeys God by looking back and paradoxically achieves immortality by being turned into a pillar of salt. This occurrence was obviously considered worthy of recording, but not so any other details about the woman — not even her own name. The same holds for the anonymous 'Pharaoh's daughter' who saved and reared the infant Moses later, in Exodus.

The second group of women are those that *are* actually named but about whom nothing, or virtually nothing is recorded, except their relationship to a significant male. Prominent in this group are Keturah, Judith, Bashermath and Zipporah — little known, possibly long forgotten characters who are recorded as doing absolutely nothing but who were, respectively, Abraham's second wife, Esau's first two wives, and Moses's wife: and there is simply nothing more we could possibly say about them.

The third group is very similar to the second group, except that the women here are not linked directly to a famous or important male figure. These women could be regarded as filling in the background. They do nothing important or memorable, but instead crop up momentarily in genealogical lists or family stories. They are very ordinary begetters, and they appear mainly as appendages to or possessions of men, often to be treated like chattels (of which more shall be said later) and commonly to be given away or sold, almost always unconsulted, by their fathers or brothers to other patriarchs in the form of masters and husbands. This group, along with the one preceding it, constitutes the vast majority of women not only in Genesis, but in the bible as a whole.

None of this is to suggest, however, that Genesis (or the rest of the bible) is totally devoid of women who are famous in their own right. Far from it. What we find, in fact, is a fourth group of women who are extremely famous for the positively nasty things they have done and the trouble they have caused, and a fifth group of women who have accomplished many fine things and whose accomplishments have been sympathetically recorded.

The fourth group contains some of the best known women in the bible. In Genesis we find Eve, and in later books the likes of Delilah and Jezebel, who have achieved fame not as Solomon or Moses did through displays of wisdom, just rule, and bravery, but rather through acts of weakness, cupidity and downright treachery. As we shall see later the bible has a marked tendency to attribute certain characteristics to women, and to cite members of this group not only as cases in point but often also in terms of analogy and generalisation (e.g., just as Eve led Adam into sin, so do all women tend to lead men astray).

Finally there is that fifth group of women whose fine qualities and noble accomplishments have been recorded in amongst the male-dominated chronicle. In Genesis we meet

Sarah, Rebekah and Rachel; and later there shall be Ruth, Naomi, Esther and Mary among others. But Mary aside, this is not an earth-shattering collection, and their doings hardly match the spectacle and grandeur of Noah, Moses, Joshua, David, Samson and Solomon, but at least their names and actions do appear. The point, however, and it is a doubly-barbed one, is that even the best of what the most highly lauded women do fades into comparative insignificance when lined up against the continuing mighty accomplishments of the leading male figures; and along with this comes the very obvious realisation, at times (as we shall see) pointed out quite explicitly in the bible, that the women in this group are small in number, a relative minority, and the exception rather than the rule.

To summarise then: in the bible it is generally the case that men judge, foretell, fight, rule and legislate — for instance, we have to read all the way to Judges 4; i.e., almost one-third of the way through the OT, before we meet our first female judge and prophet, namely Deborah — and that women are either absent altogether or else do little more than fill in the background of the biblical events, usually in the role of some man's appendage or possession. Further, it tends to be the case that women who have achieved fame have done so by employing particular 'feminine ways' in order to bring down certain men; while 'good' women are characterised as such by their faithfulness, obedience, and ability and willingness to keep the tent, rear the children, water the flock, and do as they're told. In a chronicle which is so largely devoted to battles and the establishment of legal and ethical codes it is hardly surprising that she whose role has been defined for her as the obedient hewer of wood, drawer of water, and keeper of the family tent is not going to get star billing or find herself the focus of those events which the men who have so defined her role have also considered worthy of recording and handing down.

There is, however, another far more subtle way in which women are excluded from, or at least have their presence diminished in the bible; and this is through the very language in which the bible comes to us. There is a general point to consider here, as well as a specific one.

The general point concerns the English language itself (our reference, it will be recalled, is to two English versions of the bible) which is inherently sexist in many ways, but especially so in the way that masculine forms have achieved generic status. In English it is the norm to use words such as 'mankind' almost always in a generic sense; words such as 'man' sometimes to denote the masculine ('Fred is a man') and sometimes generically ('The problems facing man today are enormous'); and words such as 'woman' *only* to denote the female (to say 'The problems facing women today are enormous' would be to refer to women's problems, not the whole of humanity's). This sort of generic use of the male form subtly, and even if without direct or conscious malice, removes or appropriates the clear specific identity of more than half of the human population, and in a sense makes them invisible. The bible, not suprisingly, continuously uses male forms generically, and in this simple way almost unnoticeably diminishes the presence of women and their importance in the historical development of the species.

The bible is, of course, anything but unusual in this regard (attempts to write and speak consistently non-sexist English are very recent and very sparse) and can thus hardly be singled out as a special target for this particular criticism: subtle appropriation of the female into male references is simply something the bible shares (and perpetuates) with virtually everything else that has ever been recorded in English.

Interestingly, however, it appears that right from the very beginning the opposite might prevail: the generic 'man' is instantly split on its very first appearance into two genders and is also specifically pluralised:

> And God said, Let us make man in our image, after our likeness: and let them have dominion over the fish of the sea, and over the fowl of the air, and over the cattle, and over all the earth . . .

> So God created man in his own image, in the image of God created he him; *male and female created he them.*
> And God blessed them . . .
>
> Genesis 1:26–8

But from there on, and right until the end of Revelation, the pluralisation and the reference to the female disappears. In general, the male form becomes generic, and gender differentiation is made only at those times when it is specifically required; e.g.:

> Now therefore kill every male among the little ones, and kill every woman that hath known man by lying with him.
>
> Numbers 31:17

The generic use of the male form appropriates women in and along with men as an 'unseen' part of the human race. However, at other places in the bible — and this is the specific point heralded above — language quite explicitly *excludes* women from the human race in that they are spoken of, in one instance along with material goods, as if they were quite separate from or additional to the general run or category of people being referred to at the particular time.

This type of exclusion, as with the generic use of male forms, is once again not unique to the bible: rather it is so commonplace that it tends to pass unnoticed until the eye is trained to find it.[3] It abounds, for instance, in school history texts written up to around a decade ago (many of which are still widely used). In one such text we read that: 'the settlers and their wives began to cultivate the land.', while in another we find that 'The pioneers took their wives and children west in wagon trains.' In such instances there is a strong even if unintended implication that men are the real settlers and pioneers, and conversely that wives and children are appendages to rather than *bona fide* settlers or pioneers. On reflection the particular authors might regret their unfortunate constructions; perhaps what we have here, and possibly in every occasion where this occurs, could be nothing more than accidental slips. That is the kindest interpretation we could place upon such constructions; but even if we allow that they are accidental slips we cannot allow that they are innocent, any more than contemporary references to 'female poets', 'lady astronauts' or 'authoresses' are completely innocent. Such constructions are reflections, expressions, or perhaps just remnants of a very real attitude and a very deeply ingrained way of thinking which continues to re-emerge and re-surface at an alarming rate. But while the history books occasionally fail to include wives among the settlers and pioneers, the bible occasionally fails to include wives and women among the very people themselves. For instance, after Abram pursues and defeats Lot's abductors:

> ... he brought back all the goods, and also brought again his brother Lot, and his goods and the women also, and the people.
> Genesis 14:16

At one point during the rebuilding of the walls of Jerusalem:

> ... there was a great cry of the people and of their wives against their brethren the Jews.
> Nehemiah 5:1

and as Christ proceeded towards Calvary:

> ... there followed him a great company of people, and of women, which also bewailed and lamented him.
> Luke 23:27

We should note, however, that just as in most of the latest history texts wives are coming to be recognised as settlers and pioneers along with the men, so too in the NEB have wives and women been at times reinstated among the people: the NEB version of the above three verses is quite beyond reproach in this regard, even though the general sense of absence and insignificance remains.

IN THE BEGINNING: WOMAN WAS CREATED INFERIOR

The notion that women are the second sex, inferior to men, begins in the bible right at the beginning: at the very creation itself. For a very short while it appears as though there could be equality between the sexes:

> And God said, Let us make man in our image, after our likeness . . .
> So God created man in his own image, in the image of God created he him; *male and female created he them.*
> Genesis 1:26–7

God didn't, however, create them simultaneously or in the same way. Adam is created first, from the very earth and God's life-breath. Eve, in fact, comes along quite a bit later. Her purpose is to help and assist the man:

> And the LORD God said, It is not good that the man should be alone; I will make him an help meet for him. [NEB — I will provide a partner for him.]
> Genesis 2:18

and her origin is not the earth and God's life-breath but rather the man himself:

> And the LORD God caused a deep sleep to fall upon Adam, and he slept: and he took one of his ribs, and closed up the flesh instead thereof:
> And the rib, which the LORD God had taken from the man, made he a woman, and brought her unto the man.
> And Adam said, This is now bone of my bones, and flesh of my flesh: she shall be called Woman, because she was taken out of Man.
> Genesis 2:21–3

And already there is enough there to be extremely suggestive that the woman is both inferior to, and shall occupy a place secondary to man. There is nothing to suggest that the woman might be superior, and even a relationship of equality would be hard to sustain on the events and the text. But as far as inferiority goes: woman is created second in time, and after Adam has undertaken certain individual accomplishments like naming all the living creatures; woman's role is described as a help meet by God; woman is literally part, and a very small part of man himself, as well as a part it hasn't affected him to lose (the appellation 'Adam's rib' is commonly applied in a derogatory manner to women, and demeaning 'Adam's rib' jokes still abound today); woman is already being referred to in the possessive case ('bone of my bone, and flesh of my flesh'); and woman, like all the other living creatures, has been named by the man.

These strains in themselves have provided sufficient justification for many to regard woman as inferior to man, and not least among those so convinced was the apostle Paul, some of whose writings shall be considered in the following section. But if all of the above can still be put away as mere suggestiveness, there is one further point in the creation story where what emerges could hardly be called suggestive; rather it is very positive and direct prescription on two fronts. After Eve is tempted, and in turn offers the forbidden fruit to Adam, God intervenes thus:

> Unto the woman he said, I will greatly multiply thy sorrow and thy conception; in sorrow thou shalt bring forth children; and thy desire shall be to thy husband, and he shall rule over thee. [NEB — he shall be your master.]
>
> Genesis 3:16

That is very explicit, and thoroughly unambiguous: within the first three chapters of the bible it is openly declared not only that the husband shall rule over the wife, but in fact more — given the context where Adam and Eve are the only humans on earth, where the institution of marriage has hardly been formalised, and where there is no possibility of things like war occurring wherein males with highly developed physical prowess might protect and defend more 'vulnerable' women and in turn gain the 'right' to dominate them — what is actually being declared is *gender* domination: that men *qua* men shall rule over women *qua* women, and all because the woman was tempted and the man was not. Thus, right from the description of the creation, the bible can be seen as prescribing, supporting and endorsing a gender differentiation in which women take an inferior place and adopt a subservient role to men. That is one front: the second is gender differentiation in terms of roles, for already they too have been prescribed — the man shall be the provider and labourer, and the woman shall be the bearer of children. And both of these roles shall be accompanied by sorrow and suffering — yet another point to be considered in more detail later.

One small point can now be added before we leave the creation, and that is that God is always referred to and depicated as male. Such reference, and it is clearly non-generic, continues right through the bible, and also permeates our entire literature, our art, and our visual perception itself: the image of God conjured up from the most ordinary of everyday thoughts through to that displayed on the ceiling of the Sistine Chapel is invariably the image of a man. The likes of Athena are not to be found in the Judeo-Christian canon, just as women always tend to miss out when forms of monotheism are revealed.[4]

THE PAULENE STATEMENTS: MAN TO COMMAND AND WOMEN TO OBEY

In four of his epistles the apostle Paul is quite forthright about what the proper role of women should be. On two occasions he seeks justification for his position in the depiction of the creation, and in doing so makes manifest the type of interpretation of the creation story which was pointed to as a distinct possibility in the previous section. First we read:

> But I would have you know, that the head of every man is Christ; and the head of the woman is the man; and the head of Christ is God.
> Every man praying or prophesying, having his head covered, dishonoureth his head.
> But every woman that prayeth or prophesieth with her head uncovered dishonoureth her head . . .
> For a man indeed ought not to cover his head, forasmuch as he is the image and glory of God: but the woman is the glory of the man.
> For the man is not of the woman; but the woman of the man.
> *Neither was the man created for the woman; but the woman for the man.*
>
> I Corinthians 11:3–9

This is tempered to some degree by the text which follows:

> Nevertheless neither is the man without the woman, neither the woman without the man, in the Lord.
> For as the woman is of the man, even so is the man also by the woman: but all things of God.[5]
>
> I Corinthians 11:11–12

But then comes a far more direct statement, this time untempered in context, and one which can hardly be ignored or 'swept under the carpet' for it occurs within a matter of lines from one of the best known even if commonly misquoted biblical aphorisms, that 'the love of money is the root of all evil'. Paul says:

> Let the woman learn in silence with all subjection.
> But I suffer not a woman to teach, nor to usurp authority over the man, but to be in silence.
> For Adam was first formed, then Eve.
> And Adam was not deceived, *but the woman being deceived was in the transgression.*

> Notwithstanding she shall be saved in childbearing, if they continue in faith and charity and holiness with sobriety.
>
> I Timothy 2:11–15

Elsewhere Paul finds his 'justification' for advocating a similar position in 'the law' (and note also the use of the possessive case):

> Let *your* women keep silence in the churches: for it is not permitted unto them to speak; but they are commanded to be under obedience, as also saith the law.
> *And if they will learn any thing, let them ask their husbands at home*: for it is a shame for women to speak in the church. [NEB — It is a shocking thing that a woman should address the congregation.]
>
> I Corinthians 14:34–5

in God's 'order of things':

> Wives, submit yourselves unto your husbands, as it is fit in the Lord. [NEB — that is your Christian duty.][6]
>
> Colossians 3:18

and through an analogy with the relationship of the church to Christ:

> Wives, submit yourselves unto your own husbands, as unto the Lord.
> For the husband is the head of the wife, even as Christ is the head of the Church: and he is the saviour of the body.
> Therefore as the church is subject unto Christ, so let the wives be to their own husbands in every thing. [NEB — just as the church is subject to Christ, so let women be to their husbands in everything.]
>
> Ephesians 5:22–4

This passage too is somewhat tempered by the text following it:

> Husbands, love your wives, even as Christ also loved the church, and gave himself for it . . .

> ... that it should be holy and without blemish.
> So ought men to love their wives as their own bodies. He that loveth his wife loveth himself...
> ... let every one of you in particular so love his wife even as himself; and the wife see that she reverence her husband.
>
> Ephesians 5:25–33

but Paul's overall position emerges as clear and consistent: even though husbands have certain obligations to their wives; even though in particular circumstances women are deserving of loving care from their husbands; and even though we are all ostensibly 'one in Christ Jesus' — women are inferior to (and weaker than) men and have been since the actual creation as well as since the first deception; women must hold their tongues and live in a submissive relationship to men; and women are to win respect and consideration through humility and subservience; while ultimately their salvation is to be found in childbearing.

Finally, it should be noted that, whereas Paul was extremely prominent in circulating such a viewpoint, he was hardly alone in his beliefs. Peter, for instance, carries the same theme along in the latter section of the NT epistles:

> Likewise, ye wives, be in subjection to your own husbands; that, if any obey not the word, they also may without the word be won by the conversation of the wives; while they behold your chaste conversation coupled with fear. [NEB — if there are any of them who disbelieve the Gospel they may be won over, without a word being said, by observing the chaste and reverent behaviour of the wives.]
>
> Whose adorning let it not be that outward adorning ... [rather] a meek and quiet spirit, which is in the sight of God of great price.
>
> For after this manner in the old time the holy women also, who trusted in God, adorned themselves, being in subjection unto their own husbands:
>
> Even as Sara obeyed Abraham, calling him Lord: whose daughters ye are, as long as ye do well, and are not afraid with any amazement.

Likewise, ye husbands, dwell with them according to knowledge, giving honour unto the wife, *as unto the weaker vessel* . . .
I Peter 3: 1–7

MAN TO COMMAND AND WIN BREAD: WOMEN TO BEAR CHILDREN

Right throughout the bible it is the norm to find men occupying the positions of authority and command. Men are the rulers, the generals, the judges, the priests and the landholders: and not, it would appear, because of their proven ability to undertake such roles or because of any proven inability among women, but rather simply because such roles are unquestionably and automatically reserved for them; conversely men are specifically designated, without argument or justification, to fill these roles. Three instances from Exodus can illustrate the recurring theme (the context of each makes it clear that the male form is not being used generically).

Moses's father-in-law realises that Moses needs help in leading and guiding the people in godly ways, and advises Moses thus:

> Moreover thou shalt provide out of all the people able *men*, such as fear God, *men* of truth, hating covetousness; and place such over them, to be rulers of thousands, and rulers of hundreds, rulers of fifties, and rulers of tens:
> And let them judge the people at all seasons . . .
> Exodus 18:21–2

And being nothing if not obedient:

> . . . Moses chose able *men* out of all Israel, and made them heads over the people, rulers of thousands, rulers of hundreds, rulers of fifties, and rulers of tens.
> Exodus 18:25

A little later God's laws and ordinances are put to the people by Moses; in one of them men are singled out especially, and this ordinance, along with many others, is repeated (possibly for emphasis). First we find:

> Three times in the year all thy males shall appear before the Lord GOD.
>
> Exodus 23:17

and then:

> Thrice in the year shall all your men children appear before the Lord GOD, the God of Israel.
>
> Exodus 34:23

Females, however, make no such appearance. Finally, the Lord commands Moses to set up the tabernacle; and then continues:

> And thou shalt bring *Aaron and his sons* unto the door of the tabernacle of the congregation, and wash them with water.
> And thou shalt put upon Aaron the holy garments, and anoint him, and sanctify him; that he may minister unto me in the priest's office.
> And thou shalt bring his *sons*, and clothe them with coats:
> And thou shalt anoint them, as thou didst anoint their father, that they may minister unto me in the priest's office: *for their anointing shall surely be an everlasting priesthood* throughout their generations.
>
> Exodus 40:12–15

Thus a state of affairs where the priesthood shall be constituted of men is set up and codified in Exodus, not just for the prevailing conditions of the time, but as a blueprint for all future generations. Women, it would appear, are meant to be quite explicitly and effectively disbarred forever: (and to this day, by and large, they continue to be disbarred in practice.)

What then of women; and also of ordinary men who will not be priests, rulers or judges? The answer is once more given in the creation story, and more particularly in God's reaction on learning that the forbidden fruit has been eaten:

> Unto the woman he said, I will greatly multiply thy sorrow and thy conception; in sorrow thou shalt bring forth children; and thy desire shall be to thy husband, and he shall rule over thee.
> And unto Adam he said, Because thou hast hearkened unto the voice of thy wife, and hast eaten of the tree, of which I commanded thee, saying, Thou shalt not eat of it: cursed is the ground for thy sake; in sorrow shalt thou eat of it all the days of thy life;
> Thorns also and thistles shall it bring forth to thee; and thou shalt eat the herb of the field;
> In the sweat of thy face shalt thou eat bread, till thou return unto the ground . . .
> Genesis 3: 16–19

It is clear here that Adam and Eve have not merely been expelled from the garden of Eden into a harsh, cruel, and sorrowful world: what has also occurred (as noted earlier) is that gender roles have been set up — man is to be, quite literally, the bread winner through physical labour (winning bread by the sweat of his brow), and woman is to be the bearer of children. And although it is not said explicitly at this point in the bible, it follows easily that she who is at home bearing and rearing children can also be gainfully employed in other household tasks like cooking, washing and cleaning, and generally serving the man; while he gets on with his work of providing and protecting, and in particular cases of judging, ruling and legislating as well. In actual fact extremely distinct gender roles have been set up; in everything that follows men are not to be found being diverted from their particular ordained tasks by having to prepare meals, clean the house, do the washing up, or look after the children; and a similar pattern of gender role differentiation is not unknown even today.

Central, then, to woman's role or place in the world, is bearing children; and it is worth noting here an interesting switch or development on this theme between its original statement and the only other reference in the bible to that original statement. In Genesis the woman is told only that she shall conceive and bring forth children in sorrow. In the hands of Paul, however, this develops into something quite different:

> And Adam was not deceived, but the woman being deceived was in the transgression.
> Notwithstanding *she shall be saved in childbearing*, if they continue in faith and charity and holiness with sobriety. [NEB — *Yet she will be saved through motherhood*, if only women continue in faith, love and holiness, with a sober mind.]
> I Timothy 2:14–15

We see, then, that childbearing (and presumably childraising) is no longer merely woman's role; it has now become her means of salvation as well.[7] It would therefore follow that women who remain childless have failed to fulfil their proper role and are in danger of not being saved, and that women who cannot have children are in some manner cursed and will be denied both personal fulfilment and salvation. The bible, at many points between Genesis and I Timothy consistently supports and reinforces such notions; and these notions are still extremely prevalent today. Pressure certainly remains upon women to have children (it is even referred to as their duty) and a stigma commonly surrounds the woman who remains childless.

Consider, for instance, the story of Rachel and Jacob. Jacob works seven years for Rachel's hand, but at the crucial moment Rachel's father, Laban, tricks Jacob and gives him Rachel's older sister, Leah, instead. The justification for this is one which has remained widespread until relatively recent times, and in some countries and sub-cultures it is still common:

> ... It must not be so done in our country, to give the younger before the firstborn.
> Genesis 29:26

Or in other words it is forbidden, or at least it is a deep shame, for a younger sister to marry before the eldest. Thus we find a restriction or law which applies to women but not to men (brothers can marry in any order); which appears incapable of having any rational basis whatsoever; and which has brought anguish, misery and degradation to untold women throughout history. (The law, and reference to the degrading practice of the older sister dancing barefoot at her younger sister's wedding, is illustrated in Shakespeare's *The Taming of the Shrew* (see especially Act II, Scene i) where the whole point of attempting to marry off Kate was so that her younger sister could marry).[8]

It is because of this restriction that Jacob finds himself married to the wrong woman, which in turn is a situation that does not please him. He then works a further seven years to gain Rachel in marriage as well, and although he loves Rachel and hates Leah he actually sleeps with them both. The results, however, are different:

> And when the LORD saw that Leah was hated, he opened her womb: but Rachel was barren.
> And Leah conceived, and bare a son . . . she said, Surely the LORD hath looked upon my *affliction*; now therefore my husband will love me.
> And she conceived again, and bare a son; and said, Because the LORD hath heard that I was hated, he hath therefore given me this son also . . .
> And she conceived again, and bare a son; and said, Now this time will my husband be joined unto me, because I have born him three sons . . .
> And she conceived again, and bare a son: and she said, Now will I praise the LORD . . .
> Genesis 29: 31–5

This continued procreation of Leah's has no recorded effect on Jacob, but it does get to Rachel in a significant way:

> And when Rachel saw that she bare Jacob no children, Rachel envied her sister; and said unto Jacob, Give me children, *or else I die*.

> And Jacob's anger was kindled against Rachel: and he said, Am I in God's stead, who hath withheld from thee the fruit of the womb?
>
> Genesis 30: 1–2

Life being meaningless and pointless for Rachel without children, she even resorts to being a surrogate mother:

> And she said, Behold my maid Bilhah, go in unto her; and she shall bear upon my knees, that I may also have children by her. [NEB — through her I may build up a family.]
>
> Genesis 30:3

The ploy works; or at least in part. Bilhah conceives two sons by Jacob; but Leah is not to be outdone and she gives Jacob her maid, Zilpah, who also bears Jacob two sons. Then Leah herself bears Jacob two more sons and a daughter. The sons are particularly significant; on account of them Leah hopes and believes Jacob will love her:

> And Leah said, God hath endued me with a good dowry; now will my husband dwell with me, because I have borne him six sons...
>
> Genesis 30:20

but soon after all finally goes well with Rachel:

> And God remembered Rachel, and God hearkened to her, and opened her womb.
> And she conceived, and bare a son; and said, *God hath taken away my reproach* [NEB — humiliation].
>
> Genesis 30: 22–3

The implication (it is actually far more than an implication) is very clear that Rachel has finally made it — that she has demonstrated her womanhood and has, with God's help, lived up to and fulfilled the basic expectations of the female of the species.

A similar, but far more generalised and metaphorical implication is to be found much later in the OT when, in the book of Hosea, Israel is rebuked for turning towards sin. Distress is promised, and is foretold in metaphors concerning infertility; barrenness is held out as the tangible sign that God has turned away; and the final image of lifelessness is couched quite specifically in feminine terms, such that infertility is connected directly to a miscarrying womb and dry breasts rather than a malfunctioning penis or diseased testicles.

> I found Israel like grapes in the wilderness; I saw your fathers as the firstripe in the fig tree at her first time: but they went to Baal-peor, and separated themselves into that shame; and their abominations were according as they loved.
> As for Ephraim, their glory shall fly away like a bird, from the birth, and from the womb, and from the conception. [NEB — no childbirth, no fruitful womb, no conceiving.]
> Though they bring up their children, yet I will bereave them, that there shall not be a man left; yea, woe also to them when I depart from them!
> ... Ephraim shall bring forth his children to the murderer.
> Give them, O LORD: what wilt thou give? give them a miscarrying womb and dry breasts.
>
> Hosea 9: 10–14

It should go without saying, of course, that apart from the most exceptional of cases (of which only one is recorded), God's good will and intervention alone are not enough to ensure that conception will take place so that woman in turn might be saved and/or fulfilled through bearing children. Also required is a healthy, in the sense of sexually potent, male — which might explain the existence of the following ordinance:

> He that is wounded in the stones, or hath his privy member cut off, shall not enter into the congregation of the LORD.
>
> Deuteronomy 23:1

Procreation, it would appear, is really at a premium. But procreation in itself does not quite seem to ensure that all will then be well for the woman. Even after producing children the mother still appears to be vulnerable in a very direct sense if the child doesn't turn out for the best. In a selection of the Proverbs the waywardness or foolishness of children is connected back directly, in one form or another, to the mother. For instance:

> A wise son maketh a glad father: but a foolish son is the heaviness of his mother.
>
> Proverbs 10:1
>
> A foolish son is a grief to his father, and bitterness to her that bare him.
>
> Proverbs 17:25

and

> The rod and reproof give wisdom: but a child left to himself bringeth his mother to shame.
>
> Proverbs 29:15

Finally, it is of particular interest to note the following list of feats (significant enough to warrant specific recording) which the Lord is deemed capable of performing, and for the performance of which praise is considered due:

> He raiseth up the poor out of the dust, and lifteth the needy out of the dunghill;
> That he may set him with princes, even with the princes of his people.
> He maketh the barren woman to keep house, and to be a joyful mother of children. Praise ye the LORD.
>
> Psalms 113: 7–9

Before offering praise, however, perhaps we might quickly glance back to the early statement that women shall bring forth children 'in sorrow'. While I cannot, of course, comment from personal experience, many of those who can have argued persuasively that sorrow should have nothing to do with it and that childbirth properly prepared for and undergone can be painless and anything but sorrowful. It is further suggested that in some of the cases where childbirth is actually painful a type of self-fulfilling prophesy could be operating: expect something to hurt and it will hurt; or since it is meant to hurt then one should actually *avoid* doing things specifically designed to alleviate the pain associated with childbirth. If there is anything in any of this then perhaps the bible may have something to answer for with regard to the pain some women do experience in childbirth. Praise seems far more warranted if *joyful* motherhood begins at, or is not traumatised by, the delivery.

WOMEN ARE COMMODITIES: TO BE GIVEN INTO MARRIAGE

The bible abounds with instances where women are literally given into marriage by their fathers, and even by their brothers, and in many of these cases the women in question are not even consulted. The following four examples illustrate the general point and also indicate some variations on the central theme.

First, consider the occasion where Abraham sends his servant to find a wife for Isaac. The servant comes upon Rebekah, who was 'very fair to look upon, a virgin . . .' (Genesis 24:16), and who proves to be a very willing servant as well. He then speaks with Rebekah's father and brother about his mission, and is told by them:

> Behold, Rebekah is before thee, take her and go, and let her be thy master's son's wife, as the LORD hath spoken.
>
> Genesis 24:51

To this stage neither Rebekah, nor her father, nor her brother had met either Abraham or Isaac; nor had Rebekah uttered a word or been given a hearing or even a chance to speak. The three men decide the issue, even though it is she who is to marry a complete stranger. The next morning she is given some degree of choice, in the matter of whether she will leave immediately or later, but not in the larger issue of whether she might or might not marry Isaac in the first place.

Next there is the case of Moses, which was settled even more easily, although in this instance Moses himself was at least present. Reuel's daughters tell their father how Moses helped them water their flock. Then:

> ... he said unto his daughters, And where is he? why is it that ye have left the man? call him that he may eat bread.
> And Moses was content to dwell with the man: and he gave Moses Zipporah his daughter.
>
> Exodus 2:20–1

In slight contrast there is the story of Jacob, Laban, Leah and Rachel, which we have encountered earlier. In this case the suitor and the father enter into a contractual arrangement for the daughter's hand; an arrangement which neither the daughter involved nor the daughter who was to become unwittingly involved has any say in. The men simply strike a bargain (it is actually struck twice) that the wages for Jacob's labour shall be Laban's daughter:

> And Laban said unto Jacob, Because thou art my brother, shouldest thou therefore serve me for nought? tell me, what shall thy wages be?
> And Laban had two daughters: the name of the elder was Leah, and the name of the younger was Rachel.
> Leah was tender eyed; but Rachel was beautiful and well favoured.
> And Jacob loved Rachel; and said, I will serve thee seven years for Rachel thy younger daughter.

The Place of Women

> And Laban said, it is better that I give her [NEB — give her] to thee, than that I should give her to another man: abide with me.
> And Jacob served seven years for Rachel . . .
> And Jacob said unto Laban, *Give me my wife* . . .
> And it came to pass in the evening, that he took Leah his daughter, and brought her to him; and he went in unto her . . .
> . . . he said unto Laban, What is this thou hast done unto me? did I not serve with thee for Rachel? wherefore then hast thou beguiled me?
> And Laban said, It must not be so done in our country, to give the younger before the firstborn.
> . . . thou shalt serve with me yet seven other years.
> And Jacob did so . . . *and he gave him Rachel* his daughter to wife also.
>
> Genesis 29:15–28

Finally there is the situation where a daughter is offered up as a prize by her father in return for a deed, virtually regardless of who it is that performs the deed and claims the prize. During the varied assaults by Judah and Simeon against the Canaanites following the death of Joshua, Kirjath-sepher becomes a target for attack — and Caleb offers an interesting incentive for its capture:

> And Caleb said, He that smiteth Kirjath-sepher, and taketh it, to him will I give Achsah my daughter to wife.
> And Othniel the son of Kenaz, Caleb's younger brother, took it: and he gave him Achsah his daughter to wife.
>
> Judges 1:12–13

And Achsah compliantly came to Othniel, asked Caleb for springs to water the land, and was not heard of again.

It should not be taken from the above instance, however, that women are always portrayed as being of such little worth that they might be given away indiscriminately. For instance, although Shechem clearly loved Dinah and offered anything that might be asked for her, she was still not given to him; for one overriding reason:

> And when Shechem the son of Hamor the Hivite, prince of the country, saw [Dinah], he took her, and lay with her, and defiled her.
> And his soul clave unto Dinah the daughter of Jacob, and he loved the damsel, and spake kindly unto the damsel.
> And Shechem spake unto his father Hamor, saying, Get me this damsel to wife . . .
> And Hamor communed with [Jacob and his sons] saying, The soul of my son Shechem longeth for your daughter: I pray you give her him to wife . . .
> And Shechem said unto her father and unto her brethren, Let me find grace in your eyes, and what ye shall say unto me I will give.
> Ask me never so much dowry and gift, and I will give according as ye shall say unto me: but give me the damsel to wife.
> And the sons of Jacob answered Shechem and Hamor his father deceitfully, and said, because he had defiled Dinah their sister:
> And they said unto them, We cannot do this thing, to give our sister to one that is uncircumcised; for that were a reproach unto us:
>
> Genesis 34:2–14

No comfort, then, for Shechem who so obviously did love Dinah, and perhaps also for Dinah, whose feelings on the matter were simply not recorded. But this incident has far more significance for us than at first meets the eye. As we shall see later, Dinah gets infinitely better treatment than three other anonymous biblical women known only as Lot's two daughters and the Levite's wife. And as we shall see immediately, Shechem was actually complying with law and custom in offering the father *post-facto* payment for a daughter's virginity.

VIOLATE THE DAUGHTER : THEN PAY THE FATHER

Virginity, as we shall see in more detail in Chapter 3, is continually held up in the bible as a highly valued feature of women. Men are advised, and at times even commanded to take virgins for wives; and women are advised, commanded and expected to retain their virginity until their wedding night. (The same expectation is not laid down explicitly for men, although there are occasional hints in this direction; e.g., in I Corinthians 6:9 fornicators — presumably unmarried ones since they are distinguished from adulterers — are listed among the 'unrighteous'). But virginity can be lost outside marriage in one of two broad ways. On the one hand women can 'play the whore' and give it up of their own desire and their own free will: an action which the bible reacts to with much unfavourable commentary and prescription. On the other hand women can be enticed and/or raped and thus lose their virginity through little or no fault of their own. In this latter case the offending male, if caught, must marry the woman he has deflowered. There is a complication, however, in that such a marriage, like all marriages, cannot take place without the consent of the woman's father. If this consent is forthcoming then all is well, and particularly so for the father who is paid a handsome bonus:

> If a man find a damsel that is a virgin, which is not betrothed, and lay hold on her, and lie with her, and they be found;
> Then the man that lay with her shall give unto *the damsel's father* fifty shekels of silver, and she shall be his wife; because he hath humbled her, he may not put her away all his days.
> Deuteronomy 22:28–9

But if this consent is not forthcoming then once again all is well — for the father. If the father withholds consent the seducer ends up poorer, the father richer, and the damsel just deflowered and dishonoured:

> And if a man entice a maid that is not betrothed, and lie with her, he shall surely endow her to be his wife.
> If her father utterly refuse to give her unto him, he shall pay money according to the dowry of virgins.
>
> Exodus 22:16–17

Similarly it is the father who is paid if a husband falsely accuses his wife of not being a virgin upon marriage:

> If any man take a wife, and go in unto her, and hate her,
> And give occasions of speech against her, and bring up an evil name upon her, and say, I took this woman, and when I came to her, I found her not a maid:
> Then shall the father of the damsel, and her mother, take and bring forth the tokens of the damsel's virginity unto the elders of the city in the gate . . .
> . . . And they shall spread the cloth before the elders of the city.
> And the elders of that city shall take that man and chastise him;
> And they shall amerce him in an hundred shekels of silver, *and give them unto the father of the damsel*, because he hath brought up an evil name upon a virgin of Israel: and she shall be his wife; he may not put her away all his days.[9]
>
> Deuteronomy 22:13–19

WOMEN ARE COMMODITIES: TO BE TAKEN, GIVEN AWAY, AND OWNED OUTSIDE OF MARRIAGE

We saw, in the section before last, how women are given into marriage, bargained for, or offered in marriage as a prize or reward for a man's performance of some deed. Marriage, however, does not appear to be the crucial factor, or even a necessary factor in the overall process of owning, giving or taking women. Women are commonly referred to in the bible as possessions, and quite often they are addressed and/or spoken of in the possessive case (e.g., 'Let *your* women keep silence in the churches . . .'; I Corinthians 14:34); but it appears that under certain circumstances they can be virtually taken and possessed at will, as part of the normal order of things. Consider, for instance, the occasion when the children of Israel defeated the Midianites and took all the Midianite women for themselves. To begin with it was as simple as this:

> And they warred against the Midianites, as the LORD commanded Moses; and they slew all the males . . .
> And the children of Israel took all the women of Midian captives, and their little ones, and took the spoil of all their cattle, and all their flocks, and all their goods.
> Numbers 31:7–9

The taking of the women comes across as nothing different from the taking of the goods and the cattle. However, on this particular occasion the children of Israel were met with a reprimand: their action incurred Moses's wrath — but perhaps not quite for the reasons we might at first suspect. Moses wasn't upset that the women were taken; what concerned him was that they were taken too indiscriminately:

> And Moses said unto them, Have ye saved all the women alive?
> Behold, these *caused* the children of Israel, through the counsel of Balaam, to commit trespass against the LORD in the matter of Peor, and there was a plague among the congregation of the LORD.
> Now therefore kill every male among the little ones, and kill every woman that hath known man by lying with him.
> But all the women children, that have not known a man by lying with him, keep alive *for yourselves*.
> Numbers 31:15–18

The theme of killing the men and taking the women — usually all the women — is a common one in the bible; and it is actually to be found spelt out and generalised as one of the laws or codes of conduct to be observed in war:

> When thou comest nigh unto a city to fight against it, then proclaim peace unto it . . .
> And if it will make no peace with thee, but will make war against thee, then thou shalt besiege it:
> And when the LORD thy God hath delivered it into thine hands, thou shalt smite every male thereof with the edge of the sword:
> But the women, and the little ones, and the cattle, and all that is in the city, even all the spoil thereof, shalt thou take unto thyself . . . [NEB — You shall put all its males to the sword, but you may take the women, the dependants, and the cattle for yourselves . . .]
> Deuteronomy 20:10–14

A small variation on this code is also laid out for those cases where the vanquisher has a particular personal desire for one of the vanquished and wishes to take her to wife. Certain rules have to be followed, and certain abuses are forbidden, but there is still an interesting let-out clause *for the man* if things don't turn out quite right for him:

> When thou goest forth to war against thine enemies, and the LORD thy God hath delivered them into thine hands, and thou hast taken them captive,
> And seest among the captives a beautiful woman, and hast a desire unto her, that thou wouldest have her to thy wife;
> Then thou shalt bring her home to thine house; and she . . .
> . . . shall remain in thine house, and bewail her father and her mother a full month: and after that thou shalt go in unto her, and be her husband, and she shall be thy wife.
> And it shall be, if thou have no delight in her [NEB — if you no longer find her pleasing], then thou shalt let her go whither she will, but thou shalt not sell her at all for money, thou shalt not make merchandise of her, because thou hast humbled her.
> Deuteronomy 21:10–14

But it is not just as the spoils of war that women may be taken and possessed. Masters, it would appear, have special rights and privileges concerning some women, even in the most peaceful of times. Masters are forbidden from owning male slaves or servants forever (unless the slave/servant freely agrees to the relationship becoming permanent); but masters can give their male slaves/servants wives, and take these wives and any children produced back, and thus re-possess them, when the male's time for freedom has come. God, it is written, told Moses to set this judgment before the people:

> If thou buy an Hebrew servant, six years shall he serve: and in the seventh he shall go out free for nothing.
> If he came in by himself, he shall go out by himself: if he were married, then his wife shall go out with him.
> If his master have given him a wife, and she have born him sons or daughters; *the wife and her children shall be her master's*, and he shall go out by himself.
>
> Exodus 21:2–4

WOMEN AS SEX OBJECTS OFFERED UP TO OTHERS

We have seen thus far that women are commonly portrayed in the bible as commodities and/or chattels to be given away, traded for, sold, taken, owned and possessed. But this is not the only way they are portrayed. There is, on the one hand, a much kinder, sympathetic, and more humane albeit distinctly patronising portrayal. But there is also, on the other hand, an extremely disturbing picture painted of woman as a sex object who can, in certain circumstances, be rightfully given over by her husband/owner (unconsulted and with no choice of her own) for the sexual use and abuse of others. The first example we meet of this is hypothetical in that the deed is proposed but not actually carried through. Job, in making a long protest of his integrity, hypothetically offers his wife to others if he has been guilty of certain transgressions.[10]

> If mine heart have been deceived by a woman, or if I have laid wait at my neighbour's door;
> Then let my wife grind unto another, and let others bow down upon her.
>
> Job 31:9–10

The next two instances, however, are anything but hypothetical, and are hardly open to alternative positive interpretations. In each case the value of a woman or women is weighed up against the duty of hospitality, and in each case the woman loses out — once with disastrous results.

The first of these incidents occurs when Lot gives lodgings and safe hospitality to two angels in the city of Sodom, and is then pressed by a mob outside to turn out his guests so that the mob might have intercourse with them. Lot refuses, possibly because homosexuality is considered an abomination (see Leviticus 20:13 among other places) but quite specifically because he cannot betray his duty as a host. Instead Lot offers the mob his two virgin daughters to do as they will with, even though virginity is supposed to be such a prized thing, and even though he is obliged to protect his daughters. The priorities are alarmingly clear, as the text demonstrates:

> And he [Lot] said, Behold now, my lords, turn in, I pray you into your servant's house, and tarry all night, and wash your feet, and ye shall rise up early, and go on your ways . . .
> . . . and they turned in unto him, and entered into his house; and he made them a feast, and did bake unleavened bread, and they did eat.
> But before they lay down, the men of the city, even the men of Sodom, compassed the house round, both old and young, all the people from every quarter:
> And they called unto Lot, and said unto him, Where are the men which came in to thee this night? bring them out unto us,

that we may know them. [NEB — so that we can have intercourse with them.]¹¹

And Lot went out at the door unto them, and shut the door after him.

And said, I pray you, brethren, *do not so wickedly*.

Behold now, I have two daughters which have not known man; let me, I pray you, bring them out unto you, and do ye to them as is good in your eyes [NEB — you can do what you like with them]: only unto these men do nothing; for therefore came they under the shadow [NEB — shelter] of my roof.

Genesis 19:2-8

The second incident concerns the Levite who goes to Bethlehem to fetch back his (anonymous) concubine/wife. The accounts of her leaving him differ from the AV to the NEB. According to the AV she 'played the whore against him', whereas in the NEB she had left him 'In a fit of anger'. Nevertheless, in each case it is reported that he went to her father's house and reclaimed her in a friendly exchange. No malice of intent is even hinted at; he seems to seriously want his wife back. However, on the way home the Levite is given shelter in Gibeah, and when the local hordes seek him out his host offers them his virgin daughter instead. This is not agreeable to the lustful crowd, so the Levite, in order to protect himself, throws his concubine/wife out to them, in what appears to be a cold and calculated manner:

So he brought him into his house, and gave provender unto the asses; and they washed their feet, and did eat and drink.

Now as they were making their hearts merry, behold, the men of the city, certain sons of Belial, beset the house round about, and beat at the door, and spake to the master of the house, the old man, saying, Bring forth the man that came into thine house, that we may know him [NEB — for us to have intercourse with him].

And the man, the master of the house, went out unto them and said unto them, Nay, my brethren, nay, I pray you, do not so wickedly; seeing that this man is come into mine house [NEB — this man is my guest], do not this folly.

> *Behold, here is my daughter a maiden, and his concubine, them I will bring out now, and humble* [NEB — *rape*] *ye them, and do with them what seemeth good unto you: but unto this man do not so vile a thing.*
>
> But the men would not hearken to him: *so the man took his concubine, and brought her forth unto them* [NEB — *thrust her outside for them*]; *and they knew her, and abused her all the night until the morning, and when the day began to spring, they let her go.*
>
> Then came the woman in the dawning of the day, and fell down at the door of the man's house where her lord was, till it was light.
>
> Judges 19:21-6

This is not the whole of it. Confronted with his dead wife/concubine the Levite cuts her up into twelve pieces and scatters her about Israel so that the whole of Israel comes to hear the story. The story, however, is very significantly truncated:

> And the men of Gibeah rose against me, and beset the house round about upon me by night, and thought to have slain me [not true — they sought intercourse]: and my concubine have they forced [no mention that she was thrust out for them], that she is dead.
>
> Judges 20:5

The children of Israel are naturally repulsed by the crime, and in return wreak merry hell against Gibeah. Interestingly, however, the deed which is decried and revenged is the mass rape: the Levite's complicity and overall treatment of his concubine/wife is never at issue (just as Lot's wickedness in offering his virgin daughters goes unnoticed as he remonstrates with the Sodomites who 'wickedly' seek his guests). The priorities, and in among them the place of women, are, as with the story of Lot in Sodom, frighteningly obvious.

As a final example we can consider a highly significant story in the bible which is, for all intents and purposes, quite like the previous two stories, even if far less violent: namely the beginnings of the rise of the house of Abraham. It goes like this.

Abraham (still named Abram at this stage) and his wife Sarai take off penniless for Egypt in order to escape the famine in their own land. The problem, however, is that Sarai is very beautiful, and Abraham fears that he will be killed by someone desiring her. He therefore determines that she shall pretend to be his sister: in this way she can be had by others while Abraham, rather than being killed, might be given favour for providing so beautiful and delicious an object. And that is exactly how it comes to be;[12] which leaves the question — was Abraham the world's first recorded pimp?

> And it came to pass, when he was come near to enter into Egypt, that he said unto Sarai his wife, Behold now, I know that thou art a fair woman to look upon:
> Therefore it shall come to pass, when the Egyptians shall see thee, that they shall say, This is his wife: and they will kill me, but they will save thee alive.
> Say, I pray thee, thou art my sister: that it may be well with me for thy sake; and my soul shall live because of thee.
> And it came to pass that, when Abram was come into Egypt, the Egyptians beheld the woman that she was very fair.
> The princes also of Pharaoh saw her, and commended her before Pharaoh: and the woman was taken into Pharaoh's house.
> And he entreated Abram well for her sake [NEB — he treated Abram well because of her] . . .
> [here the Lord intervenes; then . . .]
> . . . Pharaoh called Abram and said, What is this that thou has done unto me? why dids't thou not tell me that she was thy wife?
> Why saidst thou, She is my sister? so I might have taken her to me to wife . . . [NEB — so that I took her as a wife?]
> Genesis 12:11–19

Why indeed? Pharaoh dismisses Abram and Sarai and they leave Egypt with all their newly-acquired possessions:

> And Abram was very rich in cattle, in silver, and in gold.
> Genesis 13:2

on the basis of which he was eventually able to settle in the land of Canaan; and the rest is history!

WOMEN ARE SUB-HUMAN

It is, of course, but a short step from treating women as sex objects to treating them as sub-human creatures — and this is the way they do occasionally appear in the bible. The most notorious of incidents where this sort of thing occurs is that of the Levite and his wife, described above; and it is demonstrated most clearly in the Levite's reaction to and treatment of his wife on the morning following her horrific night. We recall that the Levite thrust his wife out for the lusting mob to rape and abuse right through the night, and after suffering this abuse she drags herself to the threshold of the door she was cast out from. The response she evoked from the husband who apparently cared for her sufficiently to travel a great distance to win her back, and who himself slept safe and sound within the house in Gibeah at her expense (how could he have slept knowing what was being done to his wife unless he regarded her as unworthy of human consideration?) is as follows:

> And her lord rose up in the morning, and opened the doors of the house, and went to go his way: and behold, the woman his concubine was fallen down at the door of the house, and her hands were upon the threshold.
> And he said unto her, *Up, and let us be going.* But none answered . . .
>
> Judges 19:27–8

WOMEN NEED MEN FOR GUIDANCE AND FULFILMENT

When Eve is created the bible tells us:

> Therefore shall a man leave his father and his mother, and shall cleave unto his wife: and they shall be one flesh.
>
> Genesis 2:24

Interestingly, however, two variously conflicting themes can be found weaving their way through the bible. First there is the negation of the above — that men just might be better off without women and by not cleaving unto a wife. This theme will be examined in more detail in Chapter 3; but at this point it can be noted that the bible never suggests that men would be totally lost or fall in a heap without women. The second theme to be found is not that men shall leave their parents and cleave unto their wives, but rather that *women* shall leave their parents and cleave unto their *husbands*. Strangely this is never stated with the directness found in Genesis 2:24; and yet right throughout the bible there are hints, suggestions and straightforward assertions that women are in some way incomplete without men, that they need men for guidance, and that they need men both to provide fulfilment and to keep them on the right track. Much of this has been seen already in the earlier consideration of woman's role as mother, as adjunct to her husband, as housekeeper and loyal servant of her husband, and as pupil and protégé of her husband ('if they will learn any thing, let them ask their husbands at home'). Nevertheless, there are other key references which make these points far more precisely and directly.

A woman's place (as we have already noted) is usually defined in the bible in relation to the man that she serves. At times this is expressed in terms of the effect she has on the man — for instance:

> A virtuous woman is a crown to her husband: but she that maketh ashamed is as rottenness in his bones.
>
> Proverbs 12:4

but it is also often expressed in terms of the effect that the man has on her, and on the performance of her role. What the role of women, both old and young, should be is laid out quite explicitly in Paul's directions to Titus:

> But speak thou the things which become sound doctrine:
> That the aged men be sober, grave, temperate, sound in faith, in charity, in patience.
> The aged women likewise, that they be in behaviour as becometh holiness, not false accusers, not given to much wine, teachers of good things;
> That they may teach the young women to be sober, to love their husbands, to love their children,
> To be discreet, chaste, keepers at home, good, obedient to their own husbands, that the word of God be not blasphemed.
> Titus 2:1–5

There is a problem however — that of actually getting the young women to act in accordance with these directions and stipulations. The young women may be back-sliding, headstrong, or simply unwilling to listen to let alone take the good advice offered them by the aged folk. In this case a stronger authority is required; and such women, it is stated, should marry (or remarry if they are young widows), become consumed by and embroiled in household duties, and generally get themselves under the guidance and control of a husband.

> Now she that is a widow indeed, and desolate, trusteth in God, and continueth in supplications and prayers night and day.
> But she that liveth in pleasure is dead while she liveth . . .
> Let not a widow be taken into the number under three score years old, having been the wife of one man,
> Well reported of for good works; if she have brought up children . . .
> But the younger widows refuse: for when they have begun to wax wanton against Christ, they will marry;
> Having damnation, because they have cast off their first faith.
> And withal they learn to be idle, wandering about from house to house; and not only idle, but tattlers also and busybodies, speaking things which they ought not.

I will therefore that the younger women marry, bear children, guide the house, give none occasion to the adversary to speak reproachfully.
For some are already turned aside after Satan.
I Timothy 5:5–15

Or in other words, marriage and a husband will straighten them out, and lead them from idleness and empty prattling (two common characteristics of women, as Chapter 3 will reveal) to the performance of good works and their proper role as child bearers and housekeepers.

There is a quaint little suggestion, however, that a new wife might not adapt easily to marriage: that she might be sad and unable to adjust on her own, and thus in the early stages could need the benefit of her husband's constant company and support. This is so serious an issue and so great could the wife's need of him be, that the husband is totally exempted from all civil duties for a year:

> When a man hath taken a new wife, he shall not go out to war, neither shall he be charged with any business: but he shall be free at home one year, and shall *cheer up* his wife which he hath taken.
> Deuteronomy 24:5

Hopefully by then she will be all right (possibly pregnant, or even a mother already), so that he might go back to a normal life.[13]

GENDER DIFFERENCES UNDER LAW AND CUSTOM

Given the different basic status and roles enjoyed by men and women in the bible it is anything but surprising to find that differences and distinctions are continually being made between them in accordance with both law and custom. These range from the most trivial of issues through to some of the more important facets of life, from the potentially reasonable to the inexplicable, and extend even as far as the animal world. And in virtually every case the female comes off worse than the male.

To begin on a trivial issue, consider hair length. When fashion decrees that men can let their hair grow long (as it did in the late 1960s) or that women might crop theirs very short (as so many did when Mia Farrow rose to fame as a movie star) possibly few who actually follow such fashion realise that they are going against the bible which has in fact spoken on the matter even if it has not ruled definitively. Paul produces a naturalistic argument in favour of there being a gender difference regarding acceptable hair length even though he recognises that nothing has yet been codified in that regard:

> Doth not even nature itself teach you, that if a man have long hair, it is a shame unto him?
> But if a woman have long hair, it is a glory to her: for her hair is given for a covering.
> But if any man seem to be contentious, we have no such custom, neither the churches of God.
> I Corinthians 11:14–16

On a far more serious note, however, the bible prescribes a gender difference with regard to the making and repudiating of vows: men are responsible for the vows they make, but vows made by a woman can be repudiated by her father and/or her husband. A lengthy quotation is required here:

> If a man vow a vow unto the LORD, or swear an oath to bind his soul with a bond; he shall not break his word, he shall do according to all that proceedeth out of his mouth.
> If a woman also vow a vow unto the LORD, and bind herself by a bond, being in her father's house in her youth;
> And her father hear her vow, and her bond wherewith she hath bound her soul, and her father shall hold his peace at her: then all

her vows shall stand, and every bond wherewith she hath bound her soul shall stand.

But if her father disallow her in the day he heareth; not any of her vows, or of her bonds wherewith she hath bound her soul, shall stand: and the LORD shall forgive her, because her father disallowed her.

And if she had at all an husband, when she vowed, or uttered ought out of her lips, wherewith she bound her soul;

And her husband heard it, and held his peace at her in the day he heard it: then her vows shall stand, and her bonds wherewith she bound her soul shall stand.

But if her husband disallowed her on the day that he heard it; then he shall make her vow, which she vowed, and that which she uttered with her lips, wherewith she bound her soul, of none effect: and the LORD shall forgive her.

But every vow of a widow, and of her that is divorced, wherewith they have bound their souls, shall stand against her.

And if she vowed in her husband's house, or bound her soul by a bond with an oath;

And her husband heard it, and held his peace at her, and disallowed her not: then all her vows shall stand, and every bond wherewith she bound her soul shall stand.

But if her husband hath utterly made them void on the day he heard them; then whatsoever proceedeth out of her lips concerning her vows, or concerning the bond of her soul shall not stand: her husband hath made them void; and the LORD shall forgive her.

Every vow, and every binding oath to afflict the soul, her husband may establish it, or her husband may make it void.

But if a husband altogether hold his peace at her from day to day; then he establisheth all her vows, or all her bonds, which are upon her: he confirmeth them, because he held his peace at her in the day that he heard them.

But if he shall any ways make them void after that he hath heard them; then he shall bear her iniquity.

Numbers 30:2–15

Women and men are also treated differently as far as inheritances are concerned. Regardless of the order of birth, things pass down automatically to the sons; and it took the test case of Mahlah and her sisters to cause the Lord to create a precedent in those cases not where a daughter is born first but only where there are no sons at all. The Lord said to Moses:

> And thou shalt speak unto the children of Israel, saying, If a man die, and have no son, then ye shall cause his inheritance to pass unto his daughter.
>
> Numbers 27:8

Actually first-born males have a very special distinction. Their rights are especially protected in Deuteronomy 21:15–17, and they are looked upon as 'the beginning of [the father's] strength' or 'the firstfruits of [the father's] manhood' (Deuteronomy 21:17). Just why it is that the first male fruit of a man's manhood should be more important than any other progeny is never made clear (perhaps it was self-evident, or requires no questioning); but the principle is taken so seriously that it is even applied to animals. First-born male animals get very special treatment, even if it is not totally to their long-term benefit:

> All the firstling males that come of thy herd and of thy flock thou shalt sanctify unto the LORD thy God: thou shalt do no work with the firstling of thy bullock, nor shear the firstling of thy sheep.
> Thou shalt eat it before the LORD thy God year by year in the place which the LORD shall choose, thou and thy household.
>
> Deuteronomy 15:19–20

The rules for freeing servants or slaves also differ in terms of whether the servant/slave in question is female or male. The full details can be found in Exodus 21; but the point can be made from a single verse; one which also silently condones and thus offers support for the practice of fathers selling their daughters into slavery:

> And if a man sell his daughter to be a maidservant, she shall

not go out as the menservants do. [NEB — When a man sells his daughter into slavery, she shall not go free as a male slave may.]
Exodus 21:7

Further gender differentiations can be seen in those areas where husbands have particular powers over their wives which the wives certainly do not have in reciprocity over their husbands. For instance, husbands can bring their wives before the priests if they merely suspect, even if only in a fit of jealousy, that infidelity might have taken place. In all such instances the women are subjected to a test — more like a public trial by ordeal — and if they are found guilty they suffer physically and become a curse among their people; but if they are found innocent then all is well for them (apart from the indignities they have endured). As for the husbands, however; first, there is no such charge or trial by ordeal which they can be made to face; and second, no guilt or blame can accrue to them even if the wife is charged in a fit of jealousy and subsequently proved to be innocent. What we have, then, is licence for men to press charges against women and have them publicly examined, but no form of recourse whatsoever for unjustly charged women.

... If any man's wife go aside, and commit a trespass against him,
And a man be with her carnally, and it be hid from the eyes of her husband, and be kept close, and she be defiled, and there be no witness against her, neither she be taken with the manner;
And the spirit of jealousy come upon him, and he be jealous of his wife, and she be defiled: *or if the spirit of jealousy come upon him, and he be jealous of his wife, and she be not defiled*:
Then shall the man bring his wife unto the priest ... [the details of the ritual/trial follow]
This is the law of jealousies, when a wife goeth aside to another instead of her husband, and is defiled;
Or when the spirit of jealousy cometh upon him, and he be jealous over his wife, and shall set the woman before the Lord, and the priest shall execute upon her all this law.

> Then shall the man be guiltless from iniquity [NEB — no guilt will attach to the husband], and this woman shall bear her iniquity.
>
> Numbers 5:12–31

After such a serious matter we might now consider one which is a little lighter but not without its significance. It seems that whenever the Lord is to be appeased with an animal sacrifice or offering, that animal must be young and without blemish (see, for instance, Leviticus 4:3–4; 4:14–15). But what we find in Leviticus 4:22–9 (among other places) is that when a priest or ruler sins and makes an offering, that offering must be a *male* animal, whereas 'if any one of the common people sin' then in this case the animal offering is to be *female*. It is as if the status of the sacrificial animal 'fits' the status of the sinner: male animals are fit sacrifices for priests and rulers, but females will do for the commoners. There seems little rational justification that might be offered for that (unless the belief that females are less worthy than males is considered to be rational).

Similarly there seems to be no possible rational justification for applying different conditions to women who have just given birth, strictly on the basis of the gender of the offspring produced. And yet the bible does just this, declaring that a mother takes twice as long to become purified when she gives birth to a daughter than she does when she gives birth to a son:[14]

> And the LORD spake unto Moses, saying,
> Speak unto the children of Israel, saying, If a woman have conceived seed, and born a man child: then she shall be unclean seven days; according to the days of the separation for her infirmity shall she be unclean . . .
> And she shall then continue in the blood of her purifying three and thirty days; she shall touch no hallowed thing, nor come into the sanctuary until the days of her purifying be fulfilled.
> But if she bear a maid child, then she shall be unclean two weeks, as in her separation: and she shall continue in the blood of her purifying three score and six days.
>
> Leviticus 12:1–5

Finally, a most intriguing gender-related law is laid down to cover cases where two men are locked in combat and the wife of one of them comes to his aid. This she is allowed to do, provided that in doing so she does not lay hold upon the 'masculinity' of his opponent; for although such an act might save her husband's life it will have been performed at considerable personal cost to the wife:

> When men strive together one with another, and the wife of the one draweth near for to deliver her husband out of the hand of him that smiteth him, and putteth forth her hand, and taketh him by the secrets:
> Then thou shalt cut off her hand, thine eye shall not pity her.
> Deuteronomy 25:11–12

It is interesting to note that nowhere in the bible are men forbidden from defending themselves or protecting others by delivering blows to an opponent's testicles, or by taking hold of their adversary's secrets. So, is what we have here a straightforward case of unabashed gender discrimination; is it open declaration of the sanctity of the male's secrets; or is it possibly even suggestive that a wife's hand is not an unreasonable price to pay for a husband's life?

NO GREATER SHAME...

Given the place in society allotted to women in the bible, and recognising especially their weakness and dependence on men, it would have to be something of a disgrace, and possibly even the ultimate shame, for a battle-seasoned male warrior to be killed by one of these females. At least that's how Abimelech saw it:

> And Abimelech came unto the tower, and fought against it, and went hard unto the door of the tower to burn it with fire.
> And a certain woman cast a piece of a millstone upon Abimelech's head, and all to brake his skull.

> Then he called hastily unto the young man his armourbearer, and said unto him, Draw thy sword, and slay me, that men say not of me, A woman slew him. And his young man thrust him through, and he died.
>
> Judges 9:52–4

So be it.

3 The Characteristics of Women

INTRODUCTION

In general, men and women are depicted quite differently in the bible, with men getting the better end of the stick by a long long way. This is hardly to suggest, however, that men are pictured, either individually or collectively, as anything like perfect beings. Far from it: individual men have their faults; and collectively cowards, liars, adulterers, rapists and fools exist in abundance among them. But there are certain highly prized human qualities that the bible picks out, like bravery, physical prowess, wisdom, fairness and piety; and these qualities seem to reside in men in vast disproportion to their occurrence and manifestation in women; whereas some women in the bible are occasionally and variously brave, strong, wise, fair and pious, the bible tends to highlight other characteristics when it comes to concentrate on women. In the bible it is much more the case that women are portrayed as stupid, as having a marked propensity to nag and prattle, as weak and cowardly, and as possessing an evil influence and power capable of leading men astray. They are also variously depicted as potentially evil, as the source of filth and sin, as the curse of the world, and even as a fate worse than death. Goodness and badness in women often comes down to their degree and range of sexual activity (virginity before and faithfulness within marriage are good); but even then there is the problem that virtually all women, including the virginal and the faithful, become unclean if not even a little repulsive one week out of each month — this unclean period itself being a direct manifestation of their particular ability to procreate, which taints their childbearing function somewhat. Finally, when the bible seeks its harshest and most disparaging analogies, women, along with their particular 'feminine characteristics', are regularly brought to the fore.

WOMEN ARE SILLY, PRATTLERS AND NAGGERS

Paul warns that in the last days there will be great wickedness on the earth, and that many men will become rather vile creatures:

> For men shall be lovers of their own selves, covetous, boasters, proud, blasphemers, disobedient to parents, unthankful, unholy.
> Without natural affection, trucebreakers, false accusers, incontinent, fierce, despisers of those that are good,
> Traitors, heady, highminded, lovers of pleasure more than lovers of God;
> Having a form of godliness, but denying the power thereof: from such turn away.
>
> II Timothy 3:2–5

But who could possibly be foolish enough to be attracted to, rather than turn away from, such men? According to Paul certain women are particularly vulnerable:

> For of this sort are they which creep into houses, and lead captive silly women laden with sins, led away with divers lusts.
> Ever learning, and never able to come to the knowledge of the truth.
> [NEB — . . .miserable women . . . burdened with a sinful past,

and led on by all kinds of desires, who are always wanting to be taught, but are incapable of reaching a knowledge of the truth.]
II Timothy 3:6–7

Earlier, Paul spells out for Timothy the sort of knowledge he should accept, and that which he should reject. In reading this advice we come upon a familiar attitude, and a most familiar phrase. Paul advises Timothy to:

> ... refuse profane and old wives' fables, and exercise thyself unto godliness. [NEB — Have nothing to do with those godless myths, fit only for old women.]
> I Timothy 4:7

The implication is extremely clear that old women talk among themselves and whip up a barrel of nonsense within their cloistered ramblings; and the disparaging phrase 'old wives' tales' is, of course, still very much with us today, describing and epitomising the opposite of truth, science and reason. So too is the phrase 'Silly old woman', its direct variants ('silly moo', etc.), and less direct but nevertheless strongly related sentiments ('as logical as an old woman's ramblings'; 'you're thinking like an old woman' etc.); all of which strongly suggest that women are basically silly, illogical and irrational (ruled by their emotions rather than reason?) and — unlike men who attain wisdom as they age — get sillier and sillier and become less amenable to reason and more susceptible to superstition as they grow older. The bible propagates this long-standing and commonly favoured notion of the rambling old woman.

In similar vein the bible also presents us with a far more sustained image of that common butt of strained humour, namely the prattling, gossiping, nagging woman. We have already seen Paul's concern with this subject; namely that women who turn away from Christ will lapse into a wanton and wasteful life characterised by idleness and gossip:

> And withal they learn to be idle, wandering about from house

to house; and not only idle, but tattlers also and busybodies, speaking things which they ought not.

I Timothy 5:13

But Paul is far from alone in recognising and highlighting that characteristic supposedly prevalent among women of simply talking too much. The book of Proverbs, for instance, has much to say about nagging wives, and the difficulties of living with them. Initially we are told that:

> ... the contentions of a wife are a continual dropping. [NEB — a nagging wife is like water dripping endlessly.]
>
> Proverbs 19:13

and this observation then undergoes considerable repetition and embellishment; for instance:

> A continual dropping in a *very* rainy day and a contentious woman are alike.
> Whosoever hideth her hideth the wind, and the ointment of his right hand, which bewrayeth itself.
> [NEB — Endless dripping on a rainy day — that is what a nagging wife is like. As well try to control the wind as to control her!
> As well try to pick up oil in one's fingers!]
>
> Proverbs 27:15–16

Understandably, then, it would be both difficult and inadvisable to have to live with such a wife. The bible tells us first that it would be better to retreat to a far corner of the house than share living space with a nagging wife:

> It is better to dwell in a corner of the housetop, than with a brawling woman in a wide house. [NEB — than have a nagging wife and a brawling household.]
>
> Proverbs 21:9

and although this particular advice is repeated virtually *ver-*

batim (Proverbs 25:24), it is also embellished somewhat and put a little more extremely in the declaration that even retreating to a quiet corner of the house may not be enough when faced with so horrendous a creature as a nagging wife. Living in the wilderness is nobody's idea of fun, and yet we are told:

> It is better to dwell in the wilderness, than with a contentious and an angry woman.
> [NEB — Better to live alone in the desert than with a nagging and ill-tempered wife.]
> Proverbs 21:19

And yet neither Proverbs, nor any other book in the bible, suggests that there might be nagging husbands who are difficult to live with, or that men, if left to themselves, will become prattlers, gossips and busybodies. These, it would appear, are distinctively feminine characteristics: and as it was indicated in the bible so too does the case continue to be propagated today. Woman may no longer be dunked for prattling as they were in mediaeval times, but the prevalence of 'gossiping women' and 'nagging wife' jokes (remove all such characters from TV situation comedies and soap operas and much of the content of TV programmes would disappear) bears searching testimony to one particular area of our prevailing beliefs — as does the minor yet quite significant point that the words 'busybody', 'prattler', 'nagger', and to recall an earlier theme, 'scatterbrain', tend to apply mainly if not exclusively to women, and have actually, if unofficially, appropriated a feminine form within themselves.

WOMEN ARE COWARDLY

In Chapter 2 we noted women being regarded as 'the weaker vessel' in relation to men (I Peter 3:7). It appears, however, that upon closer investigation women are revealed as not merely weaker than men but rather as being positively cowardly; and so much so that their actions and behaviour can be held up properly and meaningfully as analogies for cowardice, fear, loss of courage, and falling spirits.

The first suggestion of women's cowardice occurs in the creation story. God, on learning that it was the serpent who gave Eve the forbidden fruit says to the serpent:

> ... upon thy belly shalt thou go, and dust shalt thou eat all the days of thy life:
> And I will put an enmity between thee and the woman, and between thy seed and her seed ...
>
> Genesis 3:14–15

Thus it is suggested that women shall be at odds with and scared by crawling things; whereas this same state of enmity is not laid down for men.[1]

The bible, however, is far more direct than this. On the one hand there is the open assertion that women *qua* women are cowardly. For instance, in the prophecy of the destruction of Babylon and its people we read of the Chaldeans that:

> A sword is upon their horses, and upon their chariots, and upon all the mingled people that are in the midst of her; and they shall become as women ...
>
> Jeremiah 50:37

and just a little further on we also find that:

> The mighty men of Babylon have forborn to fight, they have remained in their holds: their might hath failed; they became as women ...
> [NEB — Babylon's warriors have given up the fight, they skulk in the forts;
> their courage has failed, they have become like women.]
>
> Jeremiah 51:30

On the other hand there is a more specific assertion; namely that women are especially weak and cowardly at the time of childbirth. For examples of this particular claim and/or analogy we can turn once again to the book of Jeremiah. First there is the prophecy against Moab, which shall fall thus:

> ... Behold, he shall fly as an eagle, and shall spread his wings over Moab.
> Kerioth is taken, and the strong holds are surprised, and the mighty men's hearts in Moab at that day shall be as the heart of a woman in her pangs. [NEB — the spirit of Moab's warriors shall fail like the spirit of a woman in childbirth.]
> Jeremiah 48:40–1

Then comes the turn of Edom; where very much the same sort of thing happens:

> Behold, he shall come up and fly as the eagle, and spread his wings over Bozrah: and at that day shall the heart of the mighty men of Edom be as the heart of a woman in her pangs.
> Jeremiah 49:22

With the fall of Damascus the same simile appears a third time:

> Damascus is waxed feeble, and turneth herself to flee, and fear hath seized on her: anguish and sorrows have taken her, as a woman in travail.
> Jeremiah 49:24

and finally the king of Babylon reacts in similar vein when he hears of the forces rising against him:

> The king of Babylon hath heard the report of them, and his hands waxed feeble: anguish took hold of him, and pangs as of a woman in travail.
> Jeremiah 50:43

Common contemporary statements which liken weakness or

lack of daring to the ways of women ('he carried on like a little girl', 'What are you, women or something?') and specifically to the ways of women in childbirth — losing football teams are often accused of playing like a pack of women or of displaying as much courage as expectant mothers — have a long, noble, and inspired tradition behind them.

WOMEN ARE TEMPTRESSES AND BETRAYERS

To portray women in general as cowardly is not to suggest that every woman is necessarily cowardly at all times; nor is it to foreclose the option that the occasional woman might be extremely strong in courage and capable of performing even the most daring of actions. We should not assume, therefore, either from the previous section or from all of what has been displayed up until now, that women in the bible are always passive, meek and ineffectual creatures. Most of them *are* passive, meek and ineffectual all or most of the time, but there are a number of very important exceptions. The interesting thing, however, is that when women are portrayed in the bible in active, daring, strong and influential roles they are almost always to be found stirring up mischief and/or luring some important man into trouble. In contrast to Joshua's feats at Jericho, Daniel's courage and faith in the lion's den, and Moses's parting of the Red Sea, the bible gives us instead Eve, Delilah, Jezebel and a number of regrettably anonymous women actively engaged in varying forms of temptation and betrayal.

As with many of the things so far displayed this characteristic too is first seen in the creation story where Eve is tempted, in turn tempts her husband, and subsequently leads him and the whole of humanity into transgression and suffering. Eve is weak enough to succumb to evil and temptation, but she also has that 'feminine' strength and power capable of making a man succumb to her suggestions and desires:

> And when the woman saw that the tree was good for food, and that it was pleasant to the eyes, and a tree to be desired to make one wise, she took of the fruit thereof, and did eat, and gave also unto her husband with her; and he did eat.
>
> Genesis 3:6

Now notwithstanding that he hardly appears to have put up much of a struggle, Adam is very quick and forthright in placing the blame fairly and squarely on Eve:

> And [God] said ... Hast thou eaten of the tree, whereof I commanded thee that thou shouldest not eat?
> And the man said, The woman whom thou gavest to be with me, she gave me of the tree, and I did eat.
>
> Genesis 3:11-12

And Paul, in recounting the story, also has no doubt as to where the blame really lies:

> And Adam was not deceived, but the woman being deceived was in the transgression.
>
> I Timothy 2:14

Thus Eve — the deceived and the deceiver — demonstrates here both the weakness within herself and also the strength and power which she, as a woman, can wield over man. *Fault* in the matter is clearly laid at her feet, while she is also portrayed as the *cause* of humanity's fall from grace. Both of these issues will be considered in more detail in the following section.

In what is probably one of the best known of all the biblical stories, that of Samson and Delilah, very much the same sort of thing is to be found operating: a woman, through weakness of character, is easily led into betraying a man, and then through the very strength of her 'female wiles' she is able to succeed in doing what veritable armies have failed to accomplish, until eventually she humbles the strongest of all men.

Samson, so the story goes, comes among the Philistines, to

all intents and purposes invincible; and so the Philistine lords prevail upon Delilah to betray him by finding out the source of his strength. Delilah needs little urging: a promise of eleven hundred pieces of silver from each lord quickly sets her going, and she proceeds to work upon Samson with what might now be recognised as stereotyped 'feminine ways' which are so powerful that Samson, the slayer of a thousand men with the jaw bone of an ass, is finally unable to resist. Three times Delilah asks Samson what the source of his strength is; three times he lies to her; but then Delilah plays her 'feminine' trump card and the mighty Samson, who also carried off the gates of Gaza in his arms, is undone:

> ... she said unto him, How canst thou say, I love thee, when thine heart is not with me? thou hath mocked me these three times, and hath not told me wherein thy great strength lieth.
> And it came to pass, when she pressed him daily with her words, and urged him, so that his soul was vexed unto death;
> That he told her all his heart ...
> And when Delilah saw that he had told her all his heart, she sent and called for the lords of the Philistines, saying, Come up this once, for he hath shewed me all his heart. Then the lords of the Philistines came up unto her and brought money in their hand.
> And she made him sleep upon her knees; and she called for a man, and she caused him to shave off the seven locks of his head; and she began to afflict him; and his strength went from him.
>
> Judges 16:15–19

When Joseph was in Egypt he too was landed in great misfortune through the lust, dishonesty and temptation of the anonymous wife of Potiphar, his master. Joseph, unlike Samson (and Adam), resisted and rebuffed the temptation of the evil, weak-willed woman, but she was still able to cause Potiphar to act such that Joseph ended up, unjustly, in the cells, even if his eyes were left intact:

> And it came to pass from the time that [Potiphar] had made

him overseer in his house, and over all that he had, that the LORD blessed the Egyptian's house for Joseph's sake; and the blessing of the LORD was upon all that he had in the house, and in the field . . .

. . . it came to pass after these things that his master's wife cast her eyes upon Joseph; and she said, Lie with me.

But he refused . . .

. . . how then can I do this great wickedness, and sin against God?

And it came to pass, as she spake to Joseph day by day, that he hearkened not unto her, to lie by her, or to be with her.

And it came to pass about this time that Joseph went into the house to do his business; and there was none of the men of the house there within.

And she caught him by his garment, saying, Lie with me: and he left his garment in her hand, and fled, and got him out.

And it came to pass, when she saw that he had left his garment in her hand, and was fled forth,

That she called unto the men of her house, and spake unto them, saying . . . he came in unto me to lie with me, and I cried with a loud voice . . .

. . . and he left his garment with me, and fled, and got him out . . .

And it came to pass, when his master heard the words of his wife, which she spake unto him, saying, After this manner did thy servant to me; that his wrath was kindled.

And Joseph's master took him, and put him into the prison, a place where the king's prisoners were bound: and he was there in the prison.

Genesis 39:5-20

Lot, too, was tempted and betrayed, albeit in a most unusual manner, by his (anonymous) daughters. After the destruction of Sodom and Gomorrah, and the salinisation of Lot's (anonymous) wife, Lot and his daughters go off to live in the safe isolation of the mountains. From the retreat of their mountainous cave, however, the daughters realise that neither they, nor their father, will ever lie with a stranger, and that the only possibility for them of having sexual relations, bearing children,[2] and continuing the family line rests in incest. They therefore conspire to get the deed done without Lot's knowledge, presumably because he would not have agreed to the matter. Lot is 'tempted' with wine, betrayed while in a drunken stupor, and as the text makes clear he is absolved from all agency and responsibility in the matter:

> And the firstborn said unto the younger, Our father is old, and there is not a man in the earth to come in unto us after the manner of all the earth:
> Come, let us make our father drink wine, and we will lie with him, that we may preserve seed of our father.
> And they made their father drink wine that night: and the firstborn went in, and lay with her father; and he perceived not when she lay down, nor when she arose [the same is repeated the following night with the younger daughter] . . .
> Thus were both the daughters of Lot with child by their father.
> Genesis 19:31–6

This particular story has a certain incredibility about it (and Lot's reaction to the pregnancies and childbirths is not recorded); but the important thing to note here is the theme of the women's contrivance and the man's total absolution from possible blame (and from the misfortune which ultimately plagues his descendants). A similar sort of theme underlies the story of one of the bible's most famous, or better, infamous, women — Jezebel.

Jezebel's notoriety, it would appear, far outweighs her actual evil doings, even though they are certainly not without their significance and seriousness. As we shall see in the following section it was the overall effect that she had on her husband Ahab which need concern us most about her: but here we can examine her ways in a specific situation as she applies treachery and forgery to obtain Naboth's vineyard. Ahab had sought to obtain the vineyard by legal means and had failed to do so. Learning of this, Jezebel convinces Ahab to leave it all up to her, but then employs the most devious of methods (of which Ahab appears to be completely unaware) to achieve her end:

> So she wrote letters in Ahab's name, and sealed them with his seal, and sent the letters unto the elders and to the nobles that were in his city, dwelling with Naboth.
> And she wrote in the letters, saying, Proclaim a fast, and set Naboth on high among the people:
> And set two men, sons of Belial, before him, to bear witness against him, saying, Thou didst blaspheme God and the king. And then carry him out, and stone him, that he may die.
> And the men of his city, even the elders and the nobles who were the inhabitants in his city, did as Jezebel had sent unto them, and as it was written in the letters which she had sent unto them . . .
> And it came to pass, when Jezebel heard that Naboth was stoned, and was dead, that Jezebel said to Ahab, Arise, take possession of the vineyard . . .
>
> I Kings 21:8–15

Ahab does arise, and does go forth, but as the next section shall reveal, he does not take possession of the vineyard. Rather Jezebel's evil rebounds on him, on her, and upon the whole future house of Ahab.

Ahab was, as we shall see, turned away from God by a woman. He was, however, anything but a sole victim in this regard; rather he stood among illustrious company which included even that pillar of wisdom, Solomon, who at times was so tempted and beguiled by the power and presence of women that he too turned away from God:

> But king Solomon loved many strange women . . .
> Of the nations concerning which the LORD said unto the children of Israel, Ye shall not go into them, neither shall they come in unto you: for surely *they will turn away your heart after their gods*: Solomon clave unto these in love.
> And he had seven hundred wives, princesses, and three hundred concubines: and *his wives turned away his heart.*
> For it came to pass, when Solomon was old, that his wives

turned away his heart after other gods: and his heart was not perfect with the LORD his God . . .

I Kings 11:1–5

The price Solomon paid for this was that he and his descendants lost a large section of his kingdom; and it appears, when considering all of these stories, that there is always a price to pay and some loss to be suffered. Ahab's descendants lost all of his kingdom, Lot lost his integrity, Joseph lost his freedom, Samson lost his freedom, his eyes, and his life, and Adam and his descendants lost their innocence and the chance to dwell in paradise — and all because of evil tempting women making them imperfect with the Lord. And if this could happen to one such as Solomon, then was anyone perfect with the Lord his God? We might ask: was anyone capable of resisting temptation and betrayal by women? Well, Solomon's father, David, we are told, did remain perfect and not turn away (I Kings 11:4–6), and Job too seems to qualify. When God tests Job's integrity by delivering him, conditionally, into the hands of Satan, Job is beset by much misery yet does not waver an inch. Interestingly it is his (anonymous) wife[3] who calls on Job to betray his faith, as one assumes she would have betrayed hers, in return for which advice she is branded as one of that species of 'foolish women' (whom we have met before); while Job, who so rebuked her is commended for not once sinning with his lips:

> So went Satan forth from the presence of the LORD, and smote Job with sore boils from the sole of his foot unto his crown.
> And he took him a potsherd to scrape himself withal; and he sat down among the ashes.
> Then said his wife unto him, Dost thou still retain thy integrity? curse God, and die.
> But he said unto her, Thou speakest as one of the foolish women speaketh. [NEB — You talk *as any wicked fool of a woman might talk*.] What? shall we receive good at the hand of God, and shall we not receive evil? In all this did not Job sin with his lips.
> Job 2:7–10

WOMEN ARE THE SOURCE AND CAUSE OF EVIL DOINGS

It is well that we have arrived, at this point, at the book of Job, for it is there that we find two most interesting and pertinent questions posed. First it is asked:

> What is man, that he should be clean? and he that is born of a woman, that he should be righteous?
> [NEB — What is frail man that he should be innocent, or any child of woman that he should be justified?]
> Job 15:14

and two verses later man is described as 'abominable and filthy' [NEB — 'loathsome and rotten']. A little further on a similar question is put:

> How then can man be justified with God? or how can he be clean that is born of a woman?
> [NEB — How then can a man be justified in God's sight, or one born of woman be innocent?]
> Job 25:4

and again two verses later man is described as a worm and a maggot.

The answer in both cases revolves around God's power, trust and mercy being infinite; but for our particular purpose it is the question rather than the answer which is of prime importance. Humans ('man' is being used generically), it is stated quite categorically, are abominable, filthy, loathsome, rotten and maggot-like. But why is this so? The only suggestion given at either place in either of the two chosen texts is that anything born of a woman (no generic use here) must, of necessity, be unclean, foul and pretty rotten; and by extension this results in the very direct implication that women are the source and cause of people being the horrible way they are. The texts do *not* say 'How can one be clean who is seed of man?' or 'How might mortals be justified?' — the use of 'woman' is specific and definitive, and regardless of whether such use be accidental, gratuitous or deliberate it has a distinct and unambiguous effect: the suggestion is that that which comes from a woman is pretty loathsome because it comes from a woman. This theme, which amounts to little less than a blanket condemnation of all women, recurs frequently in the bible, but not with the utmost consistency because there are some good women to consider, and also because Christ himself was born of a woman and thus there must be some grounds for exception. We shall continue to examine this suggestion that women are the source and cause of evil, filth, rottenness and transgression as this section unfolds; but here we might ask, given this blanket condemnation of all women, how much worse things might go for those caught up with women who have openly transgressed and are recognised as being particularly evil? What, for instance, should one do when confronted with an adulteress, and what effect could such a particularly fallen women have on one? The bible offers this description and advice:

> My son, attend unto my wisdom, and bow thine ear to my understanding:
> That thou mayest regard discretion, and that thy lips may keep knowledge.
> For the lips of a strange woman drop as an honeycomb, and her mouth is smoother than oil:
> But her end is bitter as wormwood, sharp as a two-edged sword.
> Her feet go down to death; her steps take hold on hell . . .
> Remove thy way far from her, and come not nigh the door of her house:
> Lest thou give thine honour unto others, and thy years unto the cruel:
> Lest strangers be filled with thy wealth; and thy labours be in the house of a stranger;
> And thou mourn at the last, when thy flesh and thy body are consumed.
> Proverbs 5:1–11

and further with regard to the strange woman (adulteress) who 'flattereth with her words':

> Let not thine heart decline to her ways, go not astray in her paths.
> For she hath cast down many wounded: yea, many strong men have been slain by her.
> Her house is the way to hell, going down to the chambers of death.
>
> Proverbs 7:24–7

The 'weaker vessel', then, appears to have quite a particular malevolent strength; and as we have seen already with Delilah her sweet words are enough of a trap to snare wayward men and lead them to their doom:

> The mouth of strange women is a deep pit: he that is abhorred of the LORD [NEB – those whom the LORD has cursed] shall fall therein.
>
> Proverbs 22:14

There is also a sense here, and in many other places as well, that certain sorts of women are deliberately and consciously lying in wait somewhere 'out there' (when spelt out specifically it is usually in the street beside their door-post) for the express purpose of snaring men and leading them astray, and eventually of destroying them completely. The sense is both naturalistic (that's the way these women are) and overtly conspiratorial; and thus the danger and the trap are portrayed as being very real and ever-present for men — as something like an ongoing power to be continuously fought against.

And yet the 'weaker vessel' is ultimately just that — the weaker vessel; both physically and morally. To illustrate the relative weakness in moral fortitude among women we need only recall the exploits of two of the anonymous ones whom we have encountered earlier. When Job is being tormented by Satan it is his wife, herself not suffering, who urges that God be denounced. And when Lot flees from Sodom it is his wife who disobeys God's command not to look back (Genesis

19:17) and is turned into a pillar of salt for her action (Genesis 19:26).

Thus far among women we have found a general cause of filth, evil and rottenness; adultresses who lure men to death and hell with sweet words; and examples of moral weakness and the tendency to disobey. Elsewhere we find certain women more bitter than death waiting (quite explicitly) as traps for sinners; while in the search for the wise upon this earth women simply fail to rate at all:

> I applied mine heart to know, and to search, and to seek out wisdom, and the reason of things, and to know the wickedness of folly, even of foolishness and madness:
> And I find more bitter than death the woman, whose heart is *snares and nets, and her hands as bands: whoso pleaseth God shall escape from her; but the sinner shall be taken by her.*
> Behold, this have I found, saith the preacher, counting one by one, to find out the account:
> Which yet my soul seeketh, but I find not: one man among a thousand have I found; but a woman among all those have I not found.
>
> Ecclesiastes 7:25–8

There is more, however; for what the bible also does, both implicitly and explicitly, is paint a picture of women as the *cause* of sinful behaviour among men, and as the cause of the downfall of certain men and the human race in general. The overall implication of this is that men (and humanity at large) could be untainted, or at the best less tainted, if it were not for the presence and actions of women. Consider, for instance, the wording of the following verses where it is quite explicitly laid out that women are the causal and active agents in bringing about transgressions among men. (The first of these is particularly interesting in that it incorporates the 'lying-in-wait' theme with the causal theme, and in doing so it indulges in some fascinating logic: even though men go to whores and adulteresses and become transgressors, it is the fault of women that men transgress — because, one supposes, it would be impossible for men to commit adultery if there were no 'loose' women around to commit adultery with. By this sort of reasoning banks could be portrayed as the cause of armed holdups; and by this sort of argument women *are* very often portrayed as the cause of the rape they have just suffered.)[4]

> For a whore is a deep ditch; and a strange woman is a narrow pit.
> She also lieth in wait as for a prey, *and increaseth the transgressors among men*.
>
> Proverbs 23:27–8

The same sort of phraseology, and implication, occurs in a passage we have examined earlier in a different context. A closer look at Moses's reaction to the Israelites' initial mercy in not killing the Midianite women reveals why his anger was so aroused; these women, so Moses claimed, had actually caused the children of Israel to transgress:

> And Moses said unto them, Have you saved all the women alive?
> Behold, these *caused* the children of Israel, through the counsel of Balaam, to commit trespass against the LORD ...
>
> Numbers 31:15–16

A very similar implication is found in the creation story. We have already seen, in Genesis 3:12 and I Timothy 2:14, how the *fault or blame* in the matter of eating the forbidden fruit and the consequent expulsion from Eden is laid squarely at Eve's feet. From here it is but a small step to regarding — and portraying — Eve as the cause of Adam's immediate downfall and subsequently of humanity's continuing sorrow; and the bible, it could be argued, actually does portray Eve in this way: the problem to sort out is whether the cause lies in Eve's speaking of the command or in Adam's obedience to it. God's words in the following quotation link the cause with

Adam, but in terms of the 'logic' identified above Adam could not have done what he did unless Eve had spoken and tempted him first.

> And unto Adam he said, *Because thou hast hearkened unto the voice of thy wife*, and hath eaten of the tree, of which I commanded thee, saying, Thou shalt not eat of it: cursed is the ground for thy sake; in sorrow shalt thou eat of it all the days of thy life.
>
> Genesis 3:17

One thing, however, is certain — namely that Adam's transgression was not just eating of the tree, but also listening to and taking notice of his wife. Perhaps this is why God sorts out the power relation between them then and there ('Unto the women he said . . . thy desire shall be to thy husband, and he shall rule over thee'; Genesis 3:16), and why Paul expressly forbids women to teach, to 'usurp' authority over men, and even to speak in churches. And it also appears that the generalisation from Adam to all of humanity is quite in order: one does not have to go too far between the lines to pick up the messages that taking notice of their wives is not a very smart thing for men to do, and that just as Eve led Adam and the whole of humanity into sin and suffering so too do all women have the propensity to bring about sin and transgression in the world. After all, what might have happened to Job if he had listened to his wife and forsaken God; and what if Lot had followed his wife's example and had a quick glance around?

At this point let us quickly reconsider the stories of Jezebel and Solomon, this time highlighting the propensity which women are pictured as having for leading men into sin and causing them to transgress.

Jezebel's overt misbehaviour, as suggested earlier, is a bit of a let down given the notoriety she has achieved. But there is more to Jezebel than mere forgery, incitement to bear false witness, and bringing about the death of an innocent man for the purpose of acquiring a miserable little vineyard. Jezebel, it would appear, had a long-lasting and pervasive effect upon her husband, Ahab, and was largely if not completely the cause of all the evil he did. Ahab is recorded as beginning to reign over Israel in I Kings 16:29. In the next verse he is reported as doing more evil than all those who had preceded him, and in the following verse his marriage to Jezebel and the beginnings of his worship of Baal are set down. Now although the wording is ambiguous it is clear that Jezebel is with him either from the very beginning or else from just after the beginning of his wicked reign. But while Jezebel is with Ahab, and causing him to do evil, Elijah is moving against Ahab, and although Elijah at one time runs foul of Jezebel he finally manages to confront Ahab — right at that very time when Ahab has gone down to take possession of Naboth's vineyard. Here, at the Lord's bidding, Elijah tells Ahab of his fate for *all* his wrongdoings, and it is further declared that Jezebel is to blame for every single one of them and not just for the evil way in which the vineyard was acquired. Jezebel is thus labelled as the cause of everything wicked that Ahab did or was: and at this point Ahab displays signs of repentance and has a certain measure of mercy cast upon him, presumably because there was some good in him, and because it was not all his fault:

> But there was none like unto Ahab, which did sell himself to work wickedness in the sight of the LORD, whom Jezebel his wife stirred up.
> And he did very abominably in following idols, according to all things as did the Amorites, whom the LORD cast out before the children of Israel. [NEB — Never was a man who sold himself to do what is wrong in the LORD's eyes as Ahab did, *and all at the prompting of Jezebel his wife.*]
>
> I Kings 21:25–6

Finally, wise old Solomon, as we have already seen, had his heart turned away from the correct path by some of his wives. This occurrence, however, was considered to be so significant by Nehemiah that he chose to make an example of it when laying down his reforms; and in the recollection the causal nature of the women's actions becomes further highlighted:

> ... Ye shall not give your daughters unto their sons, nor take their daughters unto your sons, or for yourselves. [note the give and take of daughters]
>
> Did not Solomon king of Israel sin by these things? yet among many nations was there no king like him, who was beloved of his God, and God made him king over all Israel: *Nevertheless even him did outlandish women cause to sin.* [NEB — he was loved by his God, and God made him king over all Israel; Nevertheless even he was led by foreign women into sin.]
>
> Nehemiah 13:25–6

We might wonder what hope lesser men have; and whether it just might be better for men to steer completely clear of women altogether. This issue shall be returned to later.

WOMEN HAVE PERIODS

To this stage a fairly negative picture of women is emerging from the bible; and nothing will be lost by giving away the ending — namely that it's not going to get much better. There are, as we shall see, some positive things to be said for the virtuous woman; but the virtuous woman shares one common characteristic with all other women, or at least with all women capable of procreating — the monthly period: and that in itself is seen to be a pretty dreadful state of affairs. The bible, to put it rather mildly, is not kindly disposed to menstruating women, or to any physical manifestations of menstruation such as the historical equivalent of sanitary napkins.

Consider, to begin with, Leviticus 15. Verses 2–15 deal with the rigorous means of coping with and cleansing a man who has had a discharge or issue of any sort; and the reference is clearly to abnormal and possibly contagious illnesses.

Verses 16–18 refer specifically to discharges of semen. Verses 19–24 refer directly to menstruation,[5] while verses 25–8 refer to discharges similar in nature to menstruation (one supposes, for example, spotting etc.). The substantive content of verses 19–28 is particularly significant; not only because of details like menstruating women being set apart during their periods, or the idea that things touched by a menstruating woman become unclean as well; and not only in terms of imagery and vocabulary, where words like 'unclean' and later 'sickness' are liberally used; but also as a whole — for the precautions to be taken with menstruating women, and the ritual by which they might be cleansed, are extremely similar to those set down in verses 2–15 for men who have a discharge or issue which is clearly an illness and possibly contagious. Menstruation in women seems to be put very much on a par with infectious running sores in men; and if there is one theme that emerges more clearly than any other it is the notion of uncleanliness. It would not be surprising if people who have read the following, and perhaps nothing else of significance, were to find the notion of menstruation, menstruating women themselves, and even women *per se* (since they menstruate regularly) repulsive and repugnant:

> And if a woman have an issue, and her issue in her flesh be blood, *she shall be put apart seven days*: and whosoever *toucheth* her shall be unclean until the even.[6]
> And every thing that she lieth upon in her separation [NEB — impurity] shall be unclean: every thing also that she sitteth upon shall be unclean.
> And whosoever toucheth her bed shall wash his clothes, and bathe himself in water, and be unclean until the even.
> And whosoever toucheth any thing that she sat upon shall wash his clothes, and bathe himself in water, and be unclean until the even.
> And if it be on her bed, or on any thing whereon she sitteth, when he toucheth it, he shall be unclean until the even.
> And if any man lie with her at all, and her flowers be upon him, he shall be unclean seven days; and all the bed whereon he lieth shall be unclean.

> And if a woman have an issue of her blood many days out of the time of her separation, or if it run beyond the time of her separation; [NEB — not at the time of her menstruation, or when her discharge continues beyond the period of menstruation] all the days of the issue of her uncleanness shall be as the days of her separation: she shall be unclean. [NEB — she shall be unclean as during the period of her menstruation]
>
> Every bed whereon she lieth all the days of her issue shall be unto her as the bed of her separation: and whatsoever she sitteth upon shall be unclean, as the uncleanness of her separation.
>
> And whosoever toucheth those things shall be unclean, and shall wash his clothes, and bathe himself in water, and be unclean until the even.
>
> But if she be cleansed of her issue, then she shall number to herself seven days, and after that she shall be clean.
>
> Leviticus 15:19–28

And to make it perfectly clear that the above verses are referring to menstruation, the chapter concludes thus (and in doing so introduces the concept of 'sickness' in relation to menstruation):

> This is the law of him that hath an issue, and of him whose seed goeth from him, and is defiled therewith;
>
> And of her *that is sick of her flowers,* and of him that hath an issue, of the man, and of the woman, and of him that lieth with her that is unclean.
>
> Leviticus 15:32–3

Given all of the above it is hardly surprising to find that having sexual intercourse with a menstruating woman is declared taboo; and severe penalties are imposed upon both parties engaging in such a practice: (here also the AV makes its most direct reference to menstruation being a sickness — an image which the NEB chooses not to repeat):

> And if a man shall lie with a woman having her sickness and shall uncover her nakedness; he hath discovered her fountain, and

The Characteristics of Women

she hath uncovered the fountain of her blood: and both of them shall be cut off from among their people.

Leviticus 20:18

In fact keeping one's proper distance from menstruating women is not merely one of the characteristics of a just and righteous man, but rather is significant and important enough to have been specifically short-listed by the Lord; or at least so claimed Ezekiel:

> The word of the LORD came unto me again, saying . . .
> But if a man be just, and do that which is lawful and right,
> And hath not eaten upon the mountains, neither hath lifted up his eyes to the idols of the house of Israel, neither hath defiled his neighbour's wife, *neither hath come near to a menstruous woman,*
> And hath not oppressed any, but hath restored to the debtor his pledge, hath spoiled none by violence, hath given his bread to the hungry, and hath covered the naked with a garment.
> He that hath not given forth upon usury, neither hath taken any increase, that hath withdrawn his hand from iniquity, hath executed true judgment between man and man.
> Hath walked in my statutes, and hath kept my judgments, to deal truly; he is just, he shall surely live, saith the Lord GOD.

Ezekiel 18:1–9

With such a negative attitude being displayed regularly towards menstruation and menstruating women, and with the actual menstrual blood appearing to be the definitive villain in the piece and the thing to be avoided above all else, it would not be surprising to find the bible being none too complimentary about used sanitary napkins (or their historical equivalent). Such things, it is written, must not only be carefully and thoroughly disposed of; but they also provide the basis for neat analogies and similes regarding other things which it is declared, must also be emphatically, definitively and categorically cast aside. For instance:

> Ye shall defile also the covering of thy graven images of silver,

and the ornament of thy molten images of gold: thou shalt cast them away as a menstruous cloth; thou shalt say unto it, Get thee hence.

Isaiah 30:22

(although interestingly no such direct reference is made to menstruation at this point in the NEB).

One final point about women having periods; and that is that menstruation provides one distinct centre for what is an unresolved ambivalence towards women in the bible. Menstruation, although pictured as repulsive and repugnant, as a time when women must be removed from general company and after which they must be ritually cleansed, is also the only tangible sign that women might be able to bear children and thus fulfil and save themselves, and also provide men with sons. Husbands want wives capable of bearing, and women need to bear to be fulfilled: therefore it might be expected that all would be pleased to see women displaying the sign of their fertility. Is it not strange, then, to find women being removed, spurned, and actually being referred to as 'sick' at the times when they manifest this very quality, and simultaneously demonstrate their healthiness and wellbeing?

VIRGINS ARE VIRTUOUS; WHORES ARE EVIL

It is a consistent theme in the bible that virginity before marriage and fidelity afterwards are qualities to be admired in women, and that promiscuity or 'playing the whore' at any time is to be abhorred. We have already noted some examples suggesting this in Chapter 2. For instance, after Israel defeated the Midianites, Moses insisted that the children of Israel kill all the Midianite women 'that hath known man by lying with him' and keep for themselves only the virgins. Rebekah, we recall, was chosen for Isaac in part because she was a virgin; and a long list of fathers were found commending their daughters, for one purpose or another, because their virginity had been maintained. We saw also how fathers were to be recompensed if their daughter's virginity was violated before marriage, that taking a damsel's virginity was cause enough to be forced to marry her (if the father consented), and that a man could bring his wife to trial instantly before the elders if he merely as much as suspected in a fit of jealousy that she was not a virgin when she was given to him. In this last instance we saw how the tokens of the damsel's virginity had to be laid out on view — this practice of producing the bloodstained sheets on the morning after the wedding night is still extremely common, and occurs regularly even among Christian ethnic groups in the U.K., the U.S.A. and Australia. We also saw how a man who brought false charges against a woman had to pay her father off: what we did not consider were the consequences which might befall the woman if the charges were in fact true. And the consequences, as it turns out, are very grave indeed:

> But if this thing be true, and the tokens of virginity be not found for the damsel.
> Then they shall bring out the damsel to the door of her father's house, and the *men* of her city shall stone her with stones that she die: because she hath wrought folly in Israel to play the whore in her father's house: so shalt thou put evil away from among you.
> Deuteronomy 22:20–1

Interestingly, no such law is set out for men; and also what we have here could ring with some uneasiness, for if a woman is to play the whore in her father's house it could be with some of the men of her own city who in turn might be given the task (honour? duty?) of executing her. But the whole thing is set out very directly:

> There shall be no whore of the daughters of Israel . . .
> Deuteronomy 23:17

with the moral imperative clearly gender-based.

If the preservation of virginity is such an important thing, and if women, as the weaker vessels, are at times likely to be physically unable to ward off threats to their virginity, then it would follow that those stronger males who have a vested interest in a particular woman's virginity, namely her father and brothers, should fulfil the role of protector for that woman. It would also follow that if protection failed then vengeance (even in the form of a broadsword wedding) should be sought. And so it is in the bible: fathers and brothers commonly act as protectors, and in cases where they are not successful they are commonly found seeking out vengeance. For an example where protection fails but vengeance is successfully accomplished, the story of Jacob and his sons and Shechem and Dinah can be reconsidered and followed further. It will be recalled that Shechem defiled Dinah (the daughter of Jacob) but so loved Dinah that he offered anything that might be asked for her hand in marriage. Jacob's sons utterly refused, however, because Shechem was uncircumcised. But then the trap was set. Jacob's sons 'agree' to be 'one people' with Shechem and Hamor's people, and to accede to Shechem's request, if all the Shechemite males agree to be circumcised. This they do agree to, but while they are still suffering and in pain:

> ... two of the sons of Jacob, Simeon and Levi, Dinah's brethren, took each man his sword, and came upon the city boldly, and slew all the males.
> And they slew Hamor and Shechem his son with the edge of the sword, and took Dinah out of Shechem's house, and went out.
> The sons of Jacob came upon the slain, and spoiled the city, *because they had defiled their sister.*
>
> Genesis 34:25–7

Now Jacob is a bit concerned about this. There has been deceit, treachery and bloody carnage; and he fears that he has been given a bad name and that he is highly vulnerable to counter-attack. But his sons insist that the principle justifies the means and the ends:

> ... Ye have troubled me to make me stink among the inhabitants of the land ... I being few in number, they shall gather themselves together against me, and slay me; and I shall be destroyed, I and my house.
> And they said, Should he deal with our sister as with an harlot? [NEB — Is our sister to be treated as a common whore?]
> Genesis 34:30-1

Such principles, as we have seen, were neither voiced nor acted upon by Lot, the Levite, the Levite's host, or Abraham.

Virginity is something that a woman is expected to bring to any marriage: how much more important it is then to be brought to a marriage with a priest of the people. In fact the bible strictly forbids priests from marrying a woman who has lost her virginity in any way whatsoever; even in a previous lawful and lawfully terminated marriage:

> They shall not take a wife that is a whore, or profane; neither shall they take a woman put away from her husband ...
> Leviticus 21:7

and the emphasis on virginity is spelt out even more directly with regard to the high priest:

> And he that is the high priest among his brethren ...
> ... shall take a wife in her virginity.
> A widow, or a divorced woman, or profane, or an harlot, these shall he not take: but he shall take a virgin of his own people to wife.
> Leviticus 21:10-14

Much later, in the NT, however, this 'law' or stricture is widened enormously in application, so that not merely priests or leaders but now all males are forbidden to marry women who have lost their virginity in a previous annulled marriage, on the grounds that such an action is no less than adultery:

> ... whosoever shall marry her that is divorced committeth adultery.
>
> Matthew 5:32; Matthew 19:9

One obvious result of this is that women who have been or are divorced find themselves with an unenviable situation foisted upon them. Regardless of the reason for the divorce — they may, for instance, have been subjected to terrible cruelty in their marriage — they must either remain chaste for the rest of their lives or else lead men into sin by causing them to become adulterers. This dilemma is one which perhaps they might reasonably not be expected to face, especially if they sought divorce through no fault of their own. There is also possibly a degree of arbitrariness about the whole thing, for if the women were widows rather than divorcees they could remarry without such problems: thus much seems to revolve around the apparently irrelevant matter of whether the original husband is alive or not.

Anyway; so much then for the value of virginity. At the other end of the scale lies promiscuity or whoredom, and this is so commonly and regularly denounced in the bible that the citing of examples is hardly necessary. The bible speaks out often and consistently regarding the fate of she who plays the whore; but if things are to go badly for the ordinary woman who transgresses in this way, consider perhaps with some pity the fate of the wayward daughter of a priest:

> And the daughter of any priest, if she profane herself by playing the whore, *she profaneth her father*: she shall be burnt with fire [NEB — to death].
>
> Leviticus 21:9

And so once again the evil woman is portrayed as the cause of a man's trouble and shame. But in whoredom as in most other things it appears to follow that the bigger they are (in relation to a male such as a father or a husband) the harder they fall.

THE GOOD WOMAN

Despite its predominantly negative attitude to women the bible does not deny the possibility that there can be good women in this world. How such goodness is defined, however, is another matter; and many features of the good woman have already been discovered and noted as this work has proceeded. For instance, we have seen that goodness in women tends to be measured in relation to how well they serve their husbands ('A virtuous woman is a crown to her husband: but she that maketh ashamed is as rottenness in his bones.' Proverbs 12:4), and is manifested in qualities such as loyalty, fidelity, piety and the ability to keep house and rear children properly. Good women, or good wives, must submit themselves to their husbands in all things, this being their Christian (and Jewish) duty[7] (Colossians 3:18); they must be of a meek and quiet spirit, which God ostensibly finds favourable among them (I Peter 3:4); they must be chaste and reverent, and seek and display an inner rather than an outward adorning. So much, then, for the woman who chooses to remain single or childless; for she who will not put up with whatever her husband hands out; for she who is better educated and/or knows better than her husband and corrects him when he is wrong; for she who seeks equality with rather than submission to men; and for she who will not remain meek and quiet when the time for meekness and quietness is judged past — not to mention, of course, the militant feminist, the career woman, or the woman who insists on entering male domains such as medicine, law, politics and even the clergy. Still, the good woman exists, and she is of very considerable value — but this value is also a function of her rarity; for as Spinoza reminds us '. . . all things excellent are as difficult as they are rare.'; or to parody a popular song of the 1920s, a good woman is hard to find (which is even less surprising when we consider exactly what is expected of her).

> Who can find a virtuous woman? for her price is far above rubies.
> The heart of her husband doth safely trust in her, so that he shall have no need of spoil.
> She will do him good and not evil all the days of her life.
> She seeketh wool, and flax, and worketh willingly with her hands.
> She is like the merchants' ships; she bringeth her food from afar.
> She riseth also while it is yet night, and giveth meat to her household, and a portion to her maidens.
> She considereth a field, and buyeth it: with the fruit of her hands she planteth a vineyard.
> She girdeth her loins with strength, and strengtheneth her arms.
> She perceiveth that her merchandise is good: her candle goeth not out by night.
> She layeth her hands to the spindle, and her hands hold the distaff.
> She stretcheth out her hand to the poor; yea, she reacheth forth her hands to the needy.
> She is not afraid of the snow for her household: for all her household are clothed with scarlet.
> She maketh herself coverings of tapestry; her clothing is silk and purple.
> Her husband is known in the gates, when he sitteth among the elders of the land.
> She maketh fine linen, and selleth it; and delivereth girdles unto the merchant.
> Strength and honour are her clothing; and she shall rejoice in time to come.
> She openeth her mouth with wisdom; and in her tongue is the law of kindness.
> She looketh well to the ways of her household, and eateth not the bread of idleness.

Her children arise up, and call her blessed; her husband also, and he praiseth her.

Many daughters have done virtuously, but thou excellest them all.

Favour is deceitful, and beauty is vain: but a woman that feareth the LORD, she shall be praised.

Give her of the fruit of her hands; and let her own works praise her in the gates.

Proverbs 31:10–31

WOMEN: TO HAVE OR HAVE NOT?

When we consider the negative picture painted of women virtually right throughout the bible we might expect to find somebody at some time questioning the very need for them at all, and suggesting that it might be better to do without them altogether. On the other hand, when it is recognised that without women there would be no Christ, no procreation, no future, and nobody around for the second coming (the first if you're Jewish) or the last judgment, it is obvious that it could not possibly be suggested that women might be completely put aside by all men for all times.[8] The question as to whether or not one should take a woman in marriage actually does come quite directly, and as we shall see it is answered ambivalently, just as the whole issue is treated ambivalently from Genesis onwards.

Genesis is initially clearly in favour of the existence of women, and of men teaming up with them. First God says:

> ... It is not good that the man should be alone; I will make him an help meet for him.
>
> Genesis 2:18

and then it is decreed that:

> Therefore shall a man leave his father and his mother and shall cleave unto his wife: and they shall be one flesh.
>
> Genesis 2:24

Here then is the basis for that almost isolated positive statement towards women found deep within the Proverbs:

> Whoso findeth a wife findeth a good thing, and obtaineth favour of the LORD.
>
> Proverbs 18:22

but it also becomes the basis for the dominance/subordination relationship continually posited and reiterated by Paul:

> Neither was the man created for the woman; but the woman for the man.
>
> I Corinthians 11:9

and for the recognition of woman's place in procreation and the subsequent slight mitigation in Paul's attitude:

> Nevertheless neither is the man without the woman, neither the woman without the man, in the Lord.
> For as the woman is of the man, even so is the man also by the woman; but all things of God.
>
> I Corinthians 11:11–12

It is, of course, only after the deception, and the consequent expulsion from Eden that things start to go wrong for humanity and the ambivalence towards women begins to grow. Necessary woman, who was to be good for man, is still necessary but has proved to be the cause of all man's suffering and woe. The picture from the expulsion onwards, is almost always (but by no means exclusively) that of a necessary evil. Thus, 'Whoso findeth a wife findeth a good thing' is continually implicitly qualified, and might better read 'Whoso findeth an obedient, pious, subservient wife who does not nag and carry on with silly prattle, and who is above all faithful, findeth a good thing'. And 'Who can find a virtuous woman?' emerges as a very serious question within a context where women are, as we have seen, continually portrayed as the source and cause of evil, as the seducers and betrayers of men, and in general as anything but virtuous.

There are two occasions in the bible, however, apart from where the question 'to have or have not' is put explicitly, where we get a strong suggestion that it might be better if we could do without women. On the first of these occasions we find expression of that long-standing affirmation of mateship — that the non-sexual love which can be generated between men far surpasses anything that a woman might offer a man. David, in his lament for Saul and Jonathan, says:

> I am distressed for thee, my brother Jonathan: very pleasant has thou been unto me: thy love to me was wonderful, passing the love of women.
>
> II Samuel 1:26

Such sentiments are known to pass commonly between army mates, childhood friends, and even drinking mates and business associates: and the affirmation of the superior quality of non-sexual love between men saturates western philosophy and literature — look, for instance, in the works of Plato, Oscar Wilde and that most vigorous champion of heterosexual relations, D. H. Lawrence.

The second suggestion comes in Paul's condemnation of the carnal, or lower physical life; where it is suggested that we should seek spiritual things and spiritual life rather than earthly and bodily pleasures:

> For they that are after the flesh do mind the things of the flesh; but they that are after the Spirit the things of the Spirit.
> For to be carnally minded is death; but to be spiritually minded is life and peace.
> Because the carnal mind is enmity against God: for it is not subject to the law of God, neither indeed can be.
> So then they that are in the flesh cannot please God.
>
> Romans 8:5–8

Does this mean that all carnal things, including sexual activity with women, should be completely given up? The text which follows indicates that nothing quite so drastic is being suggested for or imposed on the people; and yet the suggestion is quite clear that those who remain celibate and have nothing to do with women are in some way spiritually better, and are capable of coming nearer to and pleasing God.

The same suggestion emerges when the crucial question — to marry or not; to cleave to a wife or not — is put to Jesus by the disciples: and yet the answer carries its own vagueness and ambivalence. It appears from Jesus's answer that there are special people endowed (by God?) with a special quality of being able to transcend those earthly and physical needs and desires satisfied by women and marriage; and that through transcending such things these special people are thus able to better (or properly) serve God and the Kingdom of Heaven. The answer, then, is a rather neat one: for some it is better to marry and cleave to a wife, but for others who are able to rise above such things and get nearer to God and the Kingdom of Heaven (the potential Catholic clergy?) it is not. But what is also clear is that the latter are regarded as being an elite band; and that their way of life, which could not be practised in the disruptive and corruptive presence of women, is considered to be superior:

> His disciples say unto him, If the case of the man be so with his wife, it is not good to marry.
> But he said unto them, All men cannot receive this saying, save they to whom it is given. [NEB — That is something which not everyone can accept, but only those for whom God has appointed it.]
> For there are some eunuchs, which were born so from their mother's womb: and there are some eunuchs, which were made eunuchs of men: and there be eunuchs, which have made themselves eunuchs for the kingdom of heaven's sake. He that is able to receive it, let him receive it. [NEB — there are others who have themselves renounced marriage for the sake of the kingdom of Heaven. Let those accept it who can.]
>
> Matthew 19:10–12

The Characteristics of Women

There is one other reference point, however, at which there is no ambivalence or equivocation whatsoever. In John's vision of the end there will be 144,000 people redeemed or ransomed 'as the firstfruits of humanity for God and the Lamb'. These 144,000 will all be males, and they will all be virgins 'who did not *defile themselves with women*' and who 'have kept themselves chaste'. Those are the words of the NEB: in the AV it comes out like this:

> And I looked, and, lo, a Lamb stood on the mount Sion, and with him an hundred forty and four thousand, having his Father's name written in their foreheads.
> And I heard a voice from heaven, as the voice of many waters, and as the voice of a great thunder: and I heard the voice of harpers harping with their harps:
> And they sung as it were a new song before the throne, and before the four beasts, and the elders: and no man could learn that song but the hundred and forty and four thousand, which were redeemed from the earth.
> These are they which *were not defiled with women; for they are virgins*. These are they which follow the Lamb whithersoever he goeth. These were redeemed from among men, being the firstfruits unto God and to the Lamb.
> And in their mouth was found no guile: *for they are without fault* before the throne of God.
>
> Revelation 14:1–5

People who are concerned that the end is nigh, and who wish to be redeemed, might now consider their gender, their past and their future. Those that are male, and have not as yet defiled themselves with women, still have a chance provided that they can continue along this clearly preferable path until the appropriate time comes. But those who have known women — it has been written — will, through that action even if through no other, be with fault should they ever come before the throne of God.

SELECTED ANALOGIES WITH 'FEMALE CHARACTERISTICS'

Much of the bible was originally written in poetic form, and the AV turned it all into poetry; a large portion of the bible deals with dramatic historical events, and much of it is made up of impassioned letters. It is hardly surprising, then, to find the text of the bible bristling with metaphor, simile, personification, analogy, and other poetic and dramatic devices. What is of particular interest here, however, is the tendency within the bible to use women, factors pertaining to women, or characteristics of a supposedly feminine nature (e.g., cowardice) to make comparisons and analogies of an unfavourable nature. This tendency is so common — especially in using the image of a whore to represent just about any and every evil deed — that only selection of instances will be laid out here.

Stupidity is spoken of freely in the bible; but in Proverbs stupidity becomes a 'she', and in the NEB 'she' becomes a Lady:

> The Lady Stupidity is a flighty creature;
> the simpleton, she cares for nothing.
> She sits at the door of her house,
> on a seat in the highest part of the town,
> to invite the passers-by indoors . . .
> Proverbs 9:13–15 (NEB translation)

Not only is this blatant gender-specific personification, but within the passage are to be found other themes discussed earlier in this work; namely the notions that women are flighty, stupid, unserious and idle, and that they are to be commonly found seated as a lure or a trap waiting beside their door-posts for the unwary.

In Isaiah's prophesy about the confusion that will reign in Egypt before its covenant with Assyria and Israel is made, the weakened and disorganised country is likened in part to a drunken man, and in general to (cowardly, weak) women:

The LORD hath mingled a perverse spirit in the midst thereof: and they have caused Egypt to err in every work thereof, as a drunken man staggereth in his vomit.
Neither shall there be any work for Egypt, which the head or tail, branch or rush, may do.
In that day shall Egypt be like unto women: [NEB — the Egyptians shall become weak as women] and it shall be afraid and fear because of the shaking of the hand of the LORD of hosts, which he shaketh over it.

Isaiah 19:14–16

Similarly, when the Lord reproaches Israel and Judah for following evil and sinful ways both are referred to as females, and in long and sustained imagery both are likened in many different ways to women straying from the proper path. A sample of the complete text, which includes yet another allusion to women lying in wait for victims, must suffice here:

They say, If a man put away his wife, and she go from him, and become another man's, shall he return unto her again? shall not that land be greatly polluted? but thou hast played the harlot with many lovers; yet return again to me, saith the LORD.
Lift up thine eyes unto the high places, and see where thou hast not been lien with. In the ways hast thou sat for them . . . thou has polluted the land with thy whoredoms and with thy wickedness.
. . . thou hadst a whore's forehead, thou refused to be shamed.
. . . Hast thou seen that which backsliding Israel hath done? she is gone up upon every high mountain and under every green tree, and there hath played the harlot.
. . . And her treacherous sister Judah saw it.
And I saw, when for all the causes whereby backsliding Israel committed adultery I had put her away, and given her a bill of divorce; yet her treacherous sister Judah feared not, but went and played the harlot also.
And it came to pass through the lightness of her whoredom, that she defiled the land, and committed adultery with stones and with stocks.

> And yet for all this her treacherous sister Judah hath not turned unto me with her whole heart, but feignedly . . .
> But I said, How shall I put thee among the children [NEB — How gladly would I treat you as a *son*]; and give thee a pleasant land, a goodly heritage of the hosts of nations? and I said, Thou shalt call me, My father; and shalt not turn away from me.
> Surely as a wife treacherously departeth from her husband, so have ye dealt treacherously with me, O house of Israel, saith the LORD.
>
> Jeremiah 3:1–20

When Jeremiah laments the miserable circumstances in which Zion finds itself for having sinned, the sinner is immediately cast as a woman:

> How doth the city sit solitary, that was full of people! how is she become as a widow!. . .
>
> Lamentations 1:1

and thus the following continuing images, which connect sin and filth or repulsion with women and 'womenly' things, fit neatly together in context. For instance, we are told:

> Jerusalem hath grievously sinned; *therefore she is removed*: all that honoured her despise her, because they have seen her nakedness: yea, she sigheth, and turneth backward.
> Her filthiness is in her skirts . . .
>
> Lamentations 1:8–9

and further:

> Zion spreadeth forth her hands, and there is none to comfort her: the LORD hath commanded concerning Jacob, that his adversaries should be round about him: Jerusalem is as a menstruous woman among them.
>
> Lamentations 1:17

Actually the stigma of menstruation is raised yet again in the AV when the Lord describes Israel's once-sinful days to

Ezekiel in these terms:

> Son of man, when the house of Israel dwelt in their own land, they defiled it by their own way and by their doings: their way was before me as the uncleanness of a removed woman.
> Ezekiel 36:17

although interestingly the NEB contains no reference to women here, removed or otherwise, but refers instead to Israel's ways as being 'foul and disgusting'.

For a final example we can consider the fall of Babylon as it is set out in Revelation in a long and sustained image of the fall of an evil lecherous whore — and once more an edited version will have to suffice here:

> And there came one of the seven angels which had the seven vials, and talked with me, saying unto me, Come hither; I will show unto thee the judgment of the great whore that sitteth upon many waters:
> With whom the kings of the earth have committed fornication, and the inhabitants of the earth have been made drunk with the wine of her fornication.
> ... I saw a woman sit upon a scarlet coloured beast, full of names of blasphemy ...
> ... having a golden cup in her hand full of abominations and filthiness of her fornication.
> And upon her forehead was a name written, MYSTERY, BABYLON THE GREAT, THE MOTHER OF HARLOTS AND ABOMINATIONS OF THE EARTH.
> And I saw the woman drunken with the blood of the saints, and with the blood of the martyrs of Jesus: and when I saw her, I wondered with great admiration.
> [The angel then explains the symbolism of what has been seen, concluding:]
> And the woman which thou sawest is that great city, which reigneth over the kings of the earth.
> Revelation 17:1–18

In the following chapter of the bible the thorough and violent destruction of Babylon, still likened to an all-consuming and all-destroying woman, is detailed in a way which suggests a very clear and close comparison with Eve as temptress, and the fall and destruction of all humanity. Thus, as far as its attitude to and portrayal of women is concerned the bible can be seen as ending very much as it began. In Genesis Eve causes humanity to know of and experience evil: in Revelation, in the wreckage of the great whore that is Babylon are found the remnants of all the evil which has been done on the earth since Eve and Adam walked its surface alone:

> ... Thus with violence shall the great city Babylon be thrown down, and shall be found no more at all ...
> ... for by thy sorceries were all nations deceived.
> And in her was found the blood of prophets, and of saints, and of all that were slain upon the earth.[9]
>
> Revelation 18:21–4

4 Conclusion

It was indicated earlier that one could not play point-counterpoint with the quotations displayed in this book. But the bible is a formidable adversary, and in one tiny sweep it can, if we allow it to, lay waste everything which has here gone before. As if anticipating this sort of work, Paul warns:

> Beware lest any man spoil you through philosophy and vain deceit, after the tradition of men, after the rudiments of the world, and not after Christ.
>
> Colossians 2:8

Paul also has a description of the person and the methodology of those who might spoil you; as well as a directive as to what to do in the face of anyone who sets out against you in this way:

> If any man teach otherwise, and consent not to wholesome words, even the words of our Lord Jesus Christ, and to the doctrine which is according to godliness;
> He is proud, knowing nothing, but doting about questions and strifes of words, whereof cometh envy, strife, railings, evil surmisings,
> Perverse disputings of men of corrupt minds, and destitute of

the truth, supposing that gain is godliness: from such withdraw thyself.

I Timothy 6:3–5

And thus does the bible establish an internal defence against any attack on its own teaching and content; and in so doing it leaves each individual with the choice of either accepting that teaching or else of following perversity and corruption.

The choice is, of course, too cut and dried; and especially so with regard to the theme covered in this book.

Given the diversity of sources which make up the canon and the very lengthy time span covering the authorship of its individual books, the overall representation of women to be found there is remarkably consistent. That representation is, however, consistently condescending, patronising, derogatory, and in many places downright insulting — and it is difficult to see how such a representation could be 'according to godliness' if indeed there is a God (albeit one who moves in a mysterious way) or at least why one should be obliged to accept that sort of thing in order to *avoid* 'perverse' dispute of and with people 'of corrupt minds'.

To accept the bible as it stands, even the relatively modern NEB text, is to accept a particularly direct and overt form and expression of sexism. The bible is not 'above' sexism: rather in so far as it is a human social construct it is an integral part (possibly, as has been suggested, a most influential and pervasive part) of the social construction of gender; and consequently, given its content, it is a major factor in promulgating, reinforcing and promoting certain gender roles and divisions which are consistently demeaning and detrimental to women. It is from unthinking acceptance, and worse, from open support of such roles and divisions that we would do better to withdraw ourselves.

None of this is to say, however, that everyone who believes in the bible, or who earnestly practises Judaism or Christianity, also (and in a sense automatically) accepts and endorses the particular gender roles and divisions described in the bible. There are, in fact, a great many who daily attempt to reconcile different practices with an overriding and basic belief in the bible, and who have worked out or are in the process of working out their own individual adaptations, rationalisations and adjustments. But at the other extreme there are also a great many who proclaim various yet closely related forms of fundamentalism and in so doing promote the gender roles and divisions in question here by claiming that they have the avowed backing of divine authority.

Most people, however, fall well between these extremes, neither wrestling with the word nor vigorously championing it at the theoretic level, nor following it earnestly in practice; and for them the bible is simply a given part of the culture, the ideological framework, and the material circumstances which they inherit, reconstruct, and bequeath to future generations. But this in no way abstracts them from or diminishes their place in the continuing dynamic of historical transformation.

The whole process of assimilating our inheritance and constructing and reconstructing our present and future is one which we know far too little about; but if there is one thing we should have learnt it is that in the past we have paid far too much attention to 'significant' and 'leading' historical figures while seriously misunderstanding and underestimating the role played by what have also been badly mis-named 'the silent majority': those people without whose concurrence in both theory and practice there would have been no spreading of the ideas and material practices advocated by the likes of such 'great historical figures' as Moses, Christ or Luther.

The lives and influence of the majority of 'ordinary' people appear, on the surface, to be relatively undramatic; and yet it is these very people who are centrally implicated in and basically responsible for the establishment and propagation of cultural milieux in general; and the acceptance, realisation and promulgation of sets of beliefs, attitudes, values and practices in particular. While they might not be the people who engage most intensely with the word of the bible or who most vigorously put that word into daily practice, their life experiences are still deeply saturated in and influenced by the bible — and it is these people, along with but more than the commonly recognised seminal figures, who make history, and whose role and place in the process of historical transformation is now appearing more and more on the agenda for investigation by the social sciences.

This book has simply attempted to link up with such ongoing investigations by placing the content and influence of the bible on that same agenda; or by identifying the bible as being not only an object of academic interest for historians, linguists and theologians, but also as being of particular concern to the social sciences as they explore the areas of culture, ideology, and particularly the social construction of perception, attitudes and consciousness. How, and to what extent that agenda item is discussed, and by whom and towards what ends, are things which, rather than having been sealed in Paul's first epistle to Timothy, really now remain to be seen.

Notes

INTRODUCTION AND EXPLANATIONS

1. 'Complete' is in scare-quotes because the earliest known versions pre-date the establishment of the NT canon in AD 382.
2. Women are kept from officiating and speaking in orthodox Jewish synagogues by appeal to the divine authority of different sections of the bible, particularly Exodus 40. See below, p. 46.
3. See K. Thomas, *Religion and the Decline of Magic*, Harmondsworth: Penguin Books, 1978.
4. Orthodox Jewish women are even required to take a ritual bath following each period, and 'public' sanctified bathing places (*Mikvahs*) can still be found, even in this age of hot running water, in most cities where there is a Jewish community large enough to fund such a venture.
5. On the very day I wrote this page Mr J. Cameron read this passage from Romans in the New South Wales Legislative Assembly and then moved the motion 'That this house . . . acknowledge the Lordship of Jesus Christ and declare itself to be a legislature constituted by and responsible to God in conformity with those verses.' The motion was discussed for two hours but was not put to

the vote. For the full discussion see *Hansard* (New South Wales Legislative Assembly) for Thursday, 20 October, 1983.
6. The bible speaks continually of eternal and unchanging principles, values and prescriptions: perhaps, then, it is not surprising that it is presented and approached so commonly in an a-historic manner.
7. It is on passages such as this that a-historic readings and interpretations of the bible flourish.
8. The one exception might be that relating to taking and repudiating vows: see below pp. 70–1. None of this is to deny, of course, that many practising Christians and Jews do not accept the entire word literally, and take extreme exception to some of the laws and especially the penalties prescribed.

THE PLACE OF WOMEN

1. They are portrayed and regarded similarly in other places as well, of course. For instance, some twenty years before the appearance of the AV Shakespeare had Petruchio say of his wife:

   > I will be master of what is mine own:
   > She is my goods, my chattels; she is my house,
   > My household stuff, my field, my barn,
   > My horse, my ox, my ass, my anything...
   > *The Taming of the Shrew*, Act III, Scene ii, 226–9

   It is of interest that offence is so commonly taken to the above lines, and so rarely to those from the bible which shall be quoted as this work unfolds.
2. On the available evidence we can say between 3000 and 5000 years ago; possibly closer to the 3000 end.
3. My thanks to Gail Shelston who first made me aware of it. In forty years beforehand I had never noticed such a

construction: now I find it everywhere, even in things I had read before Gail enlightened me.
4. Popularly claimed human manifestations of the one God have been Abraham, Moses, Buddha, Zoroaster, Christ, Muhammad, Bahá'u'lláh, and even the Reverend Moon. No female in history could seriously be added to the list.
5. That the man is born of woman might not be a good thing. See below; pp. 91–2.
6. Husbands, in return, are 'required' to love their wives 'and be not bitter against them'.
7. Interestingly, the NEB *footnotes* two alternative translations: 'saved through the Birth of the Child' and 'brought safely through Childbirth'; i.e. it calls attention to them but chooses not to adopt them in the text.
8. My late mother often told me that she chose to marry my father after they arrived in Australia rather than before they left Poland, and thus also postponed their marriage for several years, in order to save her elder unmarried sister the general shame of the thing and the specific shame of having to dance barefoot at the wedding. This was in 1927.
9. After being put through that sort of degrading performance she might be none too happy to remain his wife all of her days, but she is given no option. The partial 'protection' of virginity and of women outlined in this section was a clear advance on the prevailing practices of the historical epoch in which Deuteronomy and Exodus were written, and is the sort of thing people point to in order to support the case that the bible represents progress and advancement. That much is not being challenged here: but because something is *relatively* advanced at one historical epoch does not necessarily make it good and/or desirable, either then, now, or in the future.
10. It has been argued, and most plausibly so, that Job is doing nothing of the sort: rather his 'offer' is as extreme and far-fetched as the likelihood that he has committed

the suggested transgressions. In similar vein we might swear our innocence of something on our mother's life only if we were sufficiently certain of our innocence. Nevertheless the imagery is significant.
11. There is an interesting argument propounded by some members of Gay Liberation Movements, among others, that 'know them' means precisely that, and that the Sodomites were not seeking homosexual intercourse.
12. My first religion teacher used to literally drool over this story: I will never forget his excited face saying 'Wasn't Abraham clever; wasn't Abraham clever!' I guess us kids back in the 1940s agreed at the time.
13. It sounds very altruistic and paternalistic. The NEB version, however, reads: 'He shall remain at home exempt from service for one year and *enjoy* the wife he has taken.' What a difference one little word can make: the new bride is now an object of pleasure, and the quotation better fits an earlier section.
14. The actual number of days quoted in the case of both male and female children also seems arbitrary. They seem not to relate directly even to the menstrual cycle. The 'three score and six' days associated with the female child causes chilling echoes when we come to Revelation 13:18.

THE CHARACTERISTICS OF WOMEN

1. It is, of course, the case that some women *are* scared of snakes and other 'crawlies'; and some of these women do perform with the appropriate squeals and shrieks when confronted with a crawling thing. Whether women in general are more scared than men in general is quite another point however. Also, when women squeal in fright while men attack the crawling source of fear, how

far are each merely fulfilling role expectations — expectations embedded far in the past?
2. See Chapter 2, above pp. 45–53. The need to bear children for natural and personal fulfilment is not expressed here by Lot's daughters, but the instance is yet another where women feel they simply must, by fair means or foul, produce children.
3. Job's three friends (Eliphaz, Bildad and Zophar) are named (Job 2:11); his sheep, oxen, camels and asses are counted (Job 1:3); but his wife remains 'Job's wife'.
4. Only in the first of these five examples, however, does the NEB text differ from the AV text to the extent of not proclaiming a causal relationship.
5. There have been (lame) attempts to deny this, and to claim that the verses refer to similar discharges to those covered in verses 2–15. Both common sense and the text itself lean far away from such a view — if it were so why does verse 2 not refer to 'a man or a woman', and how can verse 33 be accommodated?
6. Certain of the orthodox still never touch women other than their wives, for who can know whether a woman is menstruating or not in this brave new world wherein menstruating women are allowed to roam freely: thus the custom of making contact only through a handkerchief.
7. Women have long believed it was their *duty* to submit sexually to their husbands, or, to put it crudely (for it is crude), to lie on the bed whenever the man wanted 'satisfaction' and to seek no gratification for themselves. Until very recently it was possible to sue a deserting wife for 'Restitution of Conjugal Rights' whereby the courts ordered the wife to return, lie on the bed, and open her legs: thankfully the courts could not enforce the order.
8. A theologian of no less standing than St Thomas Aquinas is on record as claiming that women were good for one thing only — conception; and that men would do

better to seek the help or company of other men in all other endeavours. St Jerome, of the Vulgate fame, wrote vituperously of women, and his extreme attitudes could not but have helped find their way into his influential translation of the bible.

9. The reader may be surprised to have found no mention of the exploits of Salome in this book, but nobody of that name actually appears in the episode concerning the beheading of John the Baptist, as recorded in Matthew 14:1–11 and Mark 6:17–28. It is the *anonymous* daughter of Herodias who dances before Herod and extracts the fateful promise from him, but even then only at the express direction of her mother who is quite clearly the real villain in the piece. Herod is depicted largely as a man trapped by his sense of honour, and the dancer appears to be only a dutiful pawn in Herodias's evil plan to have John done away with. See especially Mark 6:22–6.

Index of Biblical Characters

Aaron 46
Abraham (also Abram) 32–3, 38, 44, 53–4, 64–5, 105, 125, 126
Abel 32
Abimelech 75–6
Achsah 55
Adam 32, 34, 39, 40, 42, 47–8, 85–6, 90, 95–6, 118
Ahab 88–90, 97
Bashermath 33
Bildad 127
Bilhah 50
Cain 32
Caleb 55
Christ 21, 24, 28, 30, 32, 38, 42, 43, 68, 79, 92, 109, 112, 117, 119, 121, 125
Daniel 84
David 35, 90, 111
Deborah 35
Delilah 34, 84–6
Dinah 55–6, 104
Elijah 97
Eliphaz 127
Enoch 32
Esau 32–3
Esther 31, 35
Eve 34, 39, 40, 42, 47, 66, 82, 84–5, 95–6, 118
Ham 32–3
Hamor 56, 104
Herod 128
Herodias 128
Isaac 32, 53–4, 102
Jacob 32, 48–50, 54–6, 104, 116
Japeth 32–3
Jezebel 34, 84, 88–9, 96–7
Job 61, 90, 93, 96, 125–6, 127
Job's wife 90, 93, 96, 127
John 32, 113
Jonathan 111
Joseph 32, 86–7, 90
Joshua 35, 55, 84
Judah 55
Judith 33
Kenaz 55
Keturah 33
Laban 48, 54–5
Leah 48–50, 54–5
Levi 104
Levite's wife (the) 56, 63–4, 66

Lot 32, 38, 62–4, 87–8, 90, 93, 96, 105
Lot's daughters 56, 62, 87–8, 127
Lot's wife 33, 87, 93–4, 96
Mahlah 72
Mary 24, 35
Moses 20, 31–5, 45–6, 54, 59, 61, 72, 74, 84, 95, 102, 121, 125
Naboth 88–9, 97
Naomi 24, 35
Noah 32–3, 35
Noah's wife 33
Othniel 55
Pharaoh's daughter 33
Potiphar 86
Rachel 35, 48–50, 54–5
Rebekah 35, 53–4, 102
Reuel 45, 54
Ruth 24, 31, 35
Salome 128
Samson 21, 35, 85–6, 90
Sarah (also Sarai) 35, 44, 65
Saul 111
Shechem 55–6, 104
Shem 32–3
Simeon 55, 104
Solomon 32, 34–5, 89–90, 96–8
Zilpah 50
Zipporah 33, 54
Zophar 127

Index of Biblical Quotations and References

Note
The books of the bible are listed here in the order in which they appear in the bible and not in alphabetical order. Chapter and verse numbers follow that of the AV.

Genesis
1:26–8; 36–7, 39
2:18; 39, 109
2:21–3; 39
2:24; 67, 109
3:6; 85
3:11–12; 85
3:12; 95
3:14–15; 82
3:16; 26, 40, 96
3:16–19; 47
3:17; 96
12:11–19; 65
13:2; 65
14:16; 38
19:2–8; 62–3
19:15; 33
19:17; 93–4
19:26; 33, 94
19:31–6; 88
24:16; 53
24:51; 53
29:15–28; 54–5
29:26; 48
29:31–5; 49
30:1–2; 49–50
30:3; 50
30:20; 50
30:22–3; 50
34:2–14; 56
34:25–7; 104
34:30–1; 105
39:5–20; 86–7

Exodus
2:20–1; 54
18:21–2; 45
18:25; 45
21:2–4; 61
21:7; 72–3
22:16–17; 58
22:18; 10–11

131

23:17; 46
34:23; 46
40:12–15; 46

Leviticus
4:3–4; 74
4:14–15; 74
4:22–9; 74
12:1–5; 74
15:2–28; 98–100
15:10; 14
15:32–3; 100
20:12; 26
20:13; 9, 14, 17, 62
20:18; 18, 100–1
21:7; 105
21:9; 106
21:10–14; 105

Numbers
5:12–31; 73–4
6:1–5; 20
27:8; 72
30:2–15; 70–1
31:7–9; 59
31:15–16; 95
31:15–18; 59
31:17; 37

Deuteronomy
15:19–20; 72
18:10; 10–11
20:10–14; 60
21:10–14; 60
21:15–17; 72
22:5; 14
22:13–19; 58
22:20–1; 103
22:28–9; 57
23:1; 51
23:17; 103
24:5; 69
25:11–12; 75

Judges
1:12–13; 55

9:52–4; 75–6
16:15–19; 86
16:17; 21
19:1–9; 16
19:21–6; 63–4
19:27–8; 66
20:5; 64

II *Samuel*
1:26; 111

I *Kings*
11:1–5; 89–90
11:4–6; 90
16:29; 97
21:8–15; 89
21:25–6; 97

Nehemiah
4:23; 16
5:1; 38
13:25–6; 98

Job
1:3; 127
2:7–10; 90
2:11; 127
15:14; 91
25:4; 91
31:9–10; 62

Psalms
113:7–9; 52

Proverbs
5:1–11; 92
7:24–7; 93
9:13–15; 114
10:1; 52
12:4; 67, 107
16:31; 19
17:25; 52
18:22; 110
19:13; 80
21:9; 80
21:19; 81
22:14; 93

Index of Biblical Quotations and References

23:27–8; 95
25:24; 80–1
27:15–16; 80
29:15; 52
31:10–31; 108–9

Ecclesiastes
7:25–8; 94
10:2; 20

Isaiah
19:14–16; 114–15
30:22; 101–2

Jeremiah
3:1–21; 115–16
48:40–1; 83
49:22; 83
49:24; 83
50:37; 82
50:43; 83
51:30; 82

Lamentations
1:1; 116
1:8–9; 116
1:17; 116

Ezekiel
18:1–9; 101
36:17; 117

Hosea
9:10–14; 51

Matthew
5:17–18; 28
5:21–2; 28
5:27–8; 28
5:32; 106
5:33–6; 28
7:3–5; 14
14:1–11; 128
19:9; 106
19:10–12; 112
19:21; 13

Mark
6:17–28; 128

Luke
23:27; 38

Romans
8:5–8; 111
13:1–6; 22–3

I *Corinthians*
6:9–10; 16–17, 26, 57
11:3–9; 42
11:9; 110
11:11–12; 42, 110
11:14; 20
11:14–16; 70
14:34; 59
14:34–5; 22, 43

Galatians
3:28; 22, 30

Ephesians
5:22–4; 43
5:25–33; 43–4

Colossians
2:8; 119
3:18; 43, 107

I *Timothy*
2:11–12; 22
2:11–15; 42–3
2:14; 85, 95
2:14–15; 48
4:7; 79
5:5–15; 68–9
5:13; 79–80
6:3–5; 119–20

II *Timothy*
3:2–5; 78
3:6–7; 78–9

Titus
2:1–5; 68

I *Peter*
3:1–7; 44–5
3:4; 107
3:7; 81

Revelation
13:18; 126
14:1–5; 113
17:1–18; 117
18:21–4; 118